The World of International Tax Planning

The World of International Tax Planning

MILTON GRUNDY M.A., of the
Inner Temple and Gray's Inn,
barrister-at-law

The right of the University of Cambridge to print and sell all manner of books was granted by Henry VIII in 1534. The University has printed and published continuously since 1584.

CAMBRIDGE UNIVERSITY PRESS

Cambridge
London New York New Rochelle
Melbourne Sydney

Published by the Press Syndicate of the University of Cambridge
The Pitt Building, Trumpington Street, Cambridge CB2 1RP
32 East 57th Street, New York, NY 10022, USA
296 Beaconsfield Parade, Middle Park, Melbourne 3206, Australia

First published 1984

Printed in Great Britain by the University Press, Cambridge

Library of Congress catalogue card number: 83–15078

British Library Cataloguing in Publication Data

Grundy, James Milton
The world of international tax planning.
1. Tax planning
I. Title
336.2 K4660

ISBN 0 521 25955 X

There is a world elsewhere

Coriolanus III.3

Contents

Preface

My imagined reader has an expertise in the taxes of his own jurisdiction – a grasp of law, a 'feel' for the way his tax authorities will approach or the Court resolve a difficulty, a capacity for an educated guess at future enactments and changes of practice. He does not expect to acquire that level of expertise in the taxes of other jurisdictions: for that he relies on telex or telephone communication with his colleagues elsewhere. But on the telex or over the telephone, he needs to be able to make an appropriate proposal to an appropriate colleague. For this purpose, there is some information he needs to have about other jurisdictions. In this book, I have set down the information which I have found most relevant in framing and explaining such proposals.

On that knife-edge between mystifying the ignorant and boring the well informed, I have tried to exclude information available elsewhere and to concentrate on being lucid about what I include. If only for the sake of my underwriters, I disclaim any intention of advising anyone as regards any particular transaction, and I make the same disclaimer on behalf of those I thank below.

I am indebted to Edo de Vries, Peter Tompkins and Tony Murty for reading the entire text in manuscript and for many useful suggestions.

I should also like to express my thanks to Richard Pease for his invaluable help in understanding the Swiss tax system and to the following for reading and amending the passages relating to their respective jurisdictions:- Andorra (D. G. MacDonald Allen); Bahamas (Donald Britchford); Bahrain (William Ballantyne); Bermuda (James Pearman); Canada (Heward Stikeman); Cayman (Ian Paget-Brown); Costa Rica (Humberto Pacheco); Cyprus (Chrysses Demetriades); Denmark (A. Lade); Germany (Juergen Killius); Gibraltar (Louis Triay); Greece (Gerasimos Vlachos); Hong Kong (Peter Edwards); Ireland (Francis

Brennan); Isle of Man (Charles Cain); Liechtenstein (Klaus Biedermann); Malaysia (M. Shankar); Monaco (Gordon Blair); Netherlands and Netherlands Antilles (Robert van de Water); Panama (Jurgen Mossak); Seychelles (Guy Riegels); Singapore (Sidney Rolt); Turks and Caicos (Seymour Gorman); U.S.A. (Marshall Langer); U.S.V.I. (Gustav Danielson). The translation into English of the Monaco Law 214 of 1936 is by Gordon Blair and is reproduced in Appendix 4 with his kind permission. The statutes contained in Appendices 3 and 5 are reprinted with the permission of the Crown.

The errors and omissions are, of course, my own unaided work.

MILTON GRUNDY

Gray's Inn, London
1 *July* 1983

Introduction

It is a truth universally acknowledged, that in all business transactions tax is a cost like any other, and, like any other, it ought to be – if the business is to remain competitive – no greater than it has to be. Where a business is conducted wholly within a single jurisdiction, this truth is often obscured, and the profitability of a domestic transaction is commonly assessed without taking tax into account. Indeed, it is not always easy to see exactly what tax ought to be taken into account: conceptually, income taxes are taxes *on* profits, not items to be deducted in computing profits. The net after-tax profit may reflect taxes or reliefs deriving from profits or losses of other accounting periods; under the United Kingdom system, the tax may be diminished or increased by capital allowances, stock relief, group relief, advance corporation tax and other items, so that the ultimate liability does not present itself as a direct business cost like wages and advertising. But, apart from this conceptual difference, there is also a practical difference between the ways of keeping down the domestic tax cost on the one hand and direct costs on the other: direct costs are a function of the way in which the business is conducted, and they are controlled by employing fewer people, lowering the advertising budget, and so on; whereas the tax cost depends primarily on other factors – on whether the business medium is a partnership, trust or company, or a group of companies, or a combination of these, on the availability of various reliefs and allowances, the extent to which the business is financed by borrowing, on the dividend policy and on other structural factors.

In international business, on the other hand, this distinction is far less pronounced. In the first place, foreign tax, unlike domestic tax, may be an item to be deducted in computing the business profit (though it may alternatively feature in the tax computation where credit for it is allowable against domestic tax), and in practice it is commonly thought of as a direct cost. A taxpayer contemplating an investment in real estate in his own country will look at the gross yield, but if the investment is to be elsewhere, he will look at the foreign tax position as part of his investment appraisal. Of course there are many exceptions to this rule, because certain domestic investments have a 'tax shelter' aspect. But in general there seems to be a much higher level of awareness of the tax consequences of international transactions, and moreover – which is in a sense another aspect of the same phenomenon – the tax consequences, both domestic and foreign, of an international transaction can be seen as a function of the way in which the transaction is carried out. So there is often the possibility of reducing the tax cost by basing the business elsewhere, or by routing it through other jurisdictions, or otherwise modifying the form of the transaction. It is these possibilities which constitute the world of international tax planning.

1. Residence

It is a general and well-recognised rule that income may be taxable in a jurisdiction either if it has its source there or if its recipient is a resident of (or incorporated in or a citizen of) that jurisdiction. Certain situations – those of the opera singer, of the peripatetic consultant, of the *rentier*, of the business whose transactions extend across frontiers – sometimes (not, by any means, always) offer the possibility of choice, both as to the location of the source and as to the residence of the recipient.

As regards the individual, three aspects of residence call for particular mention: first, the importance of not becoming resident in a jurisdiction by mistake; second, the possibility of emigrating from the jurisdiction in which he is resident; and third – perhaps the most interesting of the three – the use of temporary emigration as a tool of tax planning.

Avoiding Residence

There is little which can be said here in general terms, except to point to the problem, and to emphasise the importance of being aware of it. Typically, an individual who is a resident and citizen of, say, Australia develops what is at first a small business interest in the United States; he finds that his interests there absorb more and more of his time; at some point – and preferably sooner rather than later – he must take professional advice, to ensure that the periods of time he plans to spend there do not bring in their train any danger of his being regarded as a resident for tax purposes. The problem is most acute where it concerns what one might describe as the 'fiscally tough' countries – notably the United States, the United Kingdom and Germany (to which one should nowadays perhaps add Canada and France), where the resident taxpayer's activities outside the country are of significant importance in determining his liability to tax. Thus, if the Australian in the example accidentally acquires a U.S. residence, what will be at stake will be not merely U.S. tax on his world income, but U.S. tax on the income of non-U.S. trusts and companies which may be attributed to him under the U.S. rules.

The criteria for determining residence vary considerably, of course, from country to country. The United States, while imposing a comparatively heavy burden of tax on the 'accidental' resident[1], has for many years permitted non-resident aliens a surprising amount of physical presence within its frontiers, provided they continue to have a clear and established residence elsewhere. (But see now the stricter proposals of the Tax Simplification and Improvement Act of 1983.)The United Kingdom, by contrast, seems over-eager to pounce on the visiting foreigner, to the point where the individual who has a 'place of abode available for his use' in the United Kingdom will be regarded as resident there in any fiscal year in which he so much as sets foot in the country.

The itinerant individual must also bear in mind that by becoming resident for tax purposes in a new jurisdiction he does not necessarily cease to be resident for tax purposes in the old one. The disadvantages of dual residence may be ameliorated by a tax treaty between the two jurisdictions – the provisions for determining residence or 'fiscal domicil' and for affording residents of one country exemption from or credit for taxes in the other being designed to ensure that the same income is not taxed twice. But such relief affects only income which is covered by the treaty between the two countries concerned, and does not operate to relieve the taxpayer from tax on income arising in third countries, or an income of trusts or companies in third countries which is attributed to the taxpayer by the laws of either or both of the countries of which he is resident.

While similar considerations apply, in theory, to companies, there seems in practice less danger of a company acquiring a new residence inadvertently. A company may more commonly find that its business activities in a country give rise to a liability to tax there, but this is strictly a matter of the acquisition of a source of income and not a matter of residence. Where the problem can arise is in jurisdictions which adopt a U.K.-style test of 'management and control' in determining the residence of a company. An individual, for example, who is resident in the

United Kingdom and the owner of all the shares in an investment company which purports to be resident elsewhere may in fact exercise the true management and control himself so that the company will be regarded by the tax authorities in the United Kingdom as resident there – notwithstanding that the tax authorities in the jurisdiction in which it is incorporated or in which the directors hold their meetings may regard it as resident there and subject to tax there accordingly.

The one circumstance where it is an advantage rather than a disadvantage for a company to be treated as a resident in more than one jurisdiction is where it has an excess of deductible outgoings over its taxable income and can utilise the resulting loss for the benefit of group companies in both jurisdictions. Where, for example, a group is financed by the borrowings of a company which is a taxpayer in one jurisdiction by virtue of its place of incorporation, and in another by virtue of its place of residence, the double relief on the interest may amount (or nearly amount) to its entire cost. And a similar double deduction (see pp. 21–2) may be available in a leasing transaction, where the lessor is a taxpayer in a jurisdiction which allows depreciation to lessors, and the lessee a taxpayer in a jurisdiction which allows depreciation to lessees. One should, of course, bear in mind that the one thing a dual-resident company must avoid is income – for that is capable of being taxed in both jurisdictions (without credit in either for tax paid in the other).

The individual who acquires a second residence does not suffer any disadvantage if the jurisdiction of the second residence imposes no tax on him in consequence – for example, because it does not tax individuals, or because of some exemption applicable to him. Those who acquire a second residence because they are working in the second jurisdiction may have some advantage as regards liability to tax in the jurisdiction of their original residence – that is, if income earned abroad is more lightly taxed;[2] but this is truly an effect of the new source and not of the new residence.

Change of Residence

No doubt the most familiar feature of a high-tax jurisdiction is that those who are subject to its taxes will often consider, and may sometimes take up, the option of moving to another jurisdiction. Where a company's liability to tax depends not on its place of incorporation but on its place of residence – for example, in the United Kingdom, and many U.K. colonies and former colonies – it may find it advantageous to change its residence in anticipation of a large profit, capital gain or distribution.[3] Non-resident trustees of a settlement may be appointed in similar circumstances.[4] But while a change of residence may be appropriate for companies and trusts, it is more commonly, and indeed more conspicuously, indicated for individuals. The considerations to be borne in mind as regards the emigration of an individual is a topic about which it is extremely difficult to generalise, because each individual will be subject to the tax regime of a country in which he is already resident. There does, however, appear to be one simple generalisation which one can make, and that is, that it will always be fiscally advantageous for an individual – leaving aside the special case of the U.S. citizen – to change his residence.

Perhaps the most beneficial aspect of emigration is that the individual arrives in his new country of residence as a person without a history. If he arrives a rich man, no one is going to ask him how it came about that he is richer than he was the year before. And if he arrives a (comparatively speaking) poor man, no one is going to ask him what happened to the assets he possessed in a previous year. This is for the very good reason that the income which accrued to him before he became a taxpayer, and the capital gains he realised and the gifts he made then, are of no concern to the tax authorities in the new jurisdiction. An individual coming to a new country will want to arrive with the minimum of assets sufficient to secure him a residence permit (where such is required). Those individuals who are known to be rich will probably be well advised to arrive with wealth in excess of this minimum figure. For the rest, however, it will probably be judicious to drop off other assets *en route* from the original country of residence to the new one, the assets being located in, say, an *Anstalt* or trust or other convenient vehicle in a tax haven. In this context one should bear in mind that, for the purposes of most tax systems (Canada being the notable exception), the change of residence does not involve any notional disposition and acquisition of any capital asset, so that an immigrant does not arrive in his new country of residence with any stepped-up base for capital gains tax purposes. An interesting example of this resulted from what was known as the 'brain drain' in the 1960s. Three English scientists went to work in the United States. After a year or so, they got together with some U.S. investors and set up a corporation which, not very long afterwards (and in the way that was possible in those days), was introduced on the local stock exchange. The shares, which had cost the individuals very little, were now extremely valuable and were likely to fetch a very good price so long as they were put on the market over a period. At this point, the three scientists decided that they would like to return to England. Since the base cost for U.K. capital gains tax was low, they faced a large potential charge to tax as their shares were put on the market – a charge essentially on gains which had arisen before they became ordinarily resident in the United Kingdom. What they did therefore was to spend a brief time in a West Indies tax haven – the time, that is, after they had ceased to be resident in the United States but before they had begun to be resident in the United Kingdom. During this time they transferred their shares in the U.S. corporation to local companies in exchange for the shares, and shortly afterwards wound up these companies. By this means they acquired for U.K. tax purposes a new base cost for their U.S. shares.

A further advantage which individuals commonly obtain through emigration is an escape from gift taxes and death taxes of various kinds. Here again, an individual may leave country A a rich man and arrive in country B a (relatively) poor man, having made a variety of gifts or somehow having dropped off assets into a *Stiftung* or trust after he left country A and before he arrived in country B. The criterion of liability to capital taxes may be residence or domicil or even citizenship and, obviously, the individual will need to be advised by people expert in the laws of country A and country B. In the majority of cases, however, it can be said that one of the significant merits of emigration is a reduction of liability to capital taxes – either because the country of destination is chosen for its lack or comparative lack of capital taxes or because some kind of shedding transaction has been effected before the individual arrives in his new country of residence.

The last item to be mentioned as one of the advantages of emigration relates to exchange controls and similar currency restrictions from which the emigrant can find himself released. This is very obvious and very little need be said about it, except perhaps to stress that an individual should take care that in the process of freeing himself from one exchange control net he should not become entangled in another; for example, he should try to remain for currency purposes external to his new country of residence or, if this is not possible, he should try to keep the bulk of his investments in a vehicle which is free from exchange control restrictions.

No discussion of the question of change of residence can be complete without some reference to wholly non-fiscal aspects of emigration. It is an act to be approached with the utmost caution. In the first place, the physical move of one's earthly goods requires effort and expense comparable to that of repairing the consequences of a minor fire. But the more serious aspect of the move is the effect it can sometimes have on the personality of the individual concerned: for many, it has proved a recipe for alcoholism, divorce and premature death. Readers whose profession it is to advise in this field will be familiar with the kind of meeting with clients where both generations are present. While the son and daughter extol the charms of some exotic foreign country, with its blue skies, perpetual sunshine, swimming pools, the opportunities for the grandchildren and the beneficial effects of the climate on arthritis, one can often read in the father's face the thoughts of uprooting and of absence of former friends and familiar ways, and the prospect of uncongenial food and boring neighbours. But the children plan to inherit without the inconvenience of a government levy on father's estate and it is both surprising and depressing how often they succeed in persuading him into what can be a miserable and lonely existence in a strange place. If one is involved in advising the individual who actually has to do the moving (as opposed to advising the one or more individuals who stand to benefit financially from his doing so) then one is essentially involved in the familiar type of cost/benefit analysis inherent in this type of situation: how much tax is ne actually going to save and is it worth it? When put like that, it sounds very simple and obvious, but it is quite amazing how many people make radical changes in their lives without asking themselves that vital question.

Perhaps the most obvious advantage to be expected of a change of residence is that the emigrant should pay less tax on his future income than he has on his past income. To this end, he might move to a nil-tax or low-tax territory, but the virtues of change of residence are by no means limited to taking up residence in such countries. Any country would like to see a rich man come and live in it, and in practice most countries find some more or less discreet way to offer fiscal encouragements to such an individual to take up residence within their borders.

A list of the more obvious places to which an individual might emigrate for tax purposes appears in paragraph 17 of Appendix 1. In making his selection, an individual is bound to be influenced to some extent by climatic or political considerations, so that although he knows that there is no personal income tax in countries around the Persian Gulf or in Albania, he will nevertheless confine himself to the more conventional destinations. The more inviting of these are considered in the following pages.

Andorra is a gateway to Spain and may be reached from either France or Spain. The oldest state in Europe, it is a quasi-autonomous Co-Principality, with a thirty-two-member General Council, a President and an inner Cabinet, and two Co-Princes, Spanish and French. The language is Catalan, but French and Spanish are in everyday use. There is no general income tax and none is proposed, nor are there capital taxes or death duties. The Principality has no international debts; there are no political parties and there is the very minimum of government. Government revenue is derived from a small import duty. An individual wishing to spend time in France, Portugal or Spain may establish his domicil or base in Andorra and a foreigner can own one apartment or a chalet. Small annual property taxes are payable to the local Comú or town hall. The cost of living is substantially lower than France or Spain, but good property and land is dear. At La Seu d'Urgell the new airport is now open. The climate is generally mild and dry, although, of course, in the ski areas there is winter snow. Surprisingly, the Principality is a tobacco-growing country and boasts the world's largest cigars.

Antigua taxes companies, but not individuals. Of the zero-tax territories, the Bahamas is much the most plausible as a place of residence. It is especially convenient for individuals who want to visit the United States but do not want to become resident there. The attractions of Monte Carlo are well known. A residence visa is required, and the Principality takes active steps to discourage foreigners who do not actually reside in their residences. Although there is no personal income tax, Monaco has French-style value added tax; it is part of the French franc zone so that residents are subject to French exchange control (which, however, now permits foreigners to retain and vary their external funds and to operate foreign bank accounts, and which no longer requires them to remit their foreign income). The cost of living is not as high as one might suppose, but property is very expensive.

Certain countries offer special tax incentives to encourage new residents. Cyprus offers aliens some small reductions in tax rates. Also, it still has a 'remittance basis' similar to that of the United Kingdom – as have several other places with a historical connection with Britain – the British Virgin Islands, for example. There are exemptions for 'creative' individuals who settle in Ireland, and wider exemptions for foreigners who go to live in Sri Lanka. Countries with a territorial basis of taxation have an obvious attraction for individuals whose investments are elsewhere.

Of these Costa Rica has the special attraction that it is one of the few places – indeed perhaps the only place – in the world where a foreigner can obtain a passport. Countries with low tax rates have similarly obvious attractions, especially since individuals who are resident there may often obtain the benefit of tax treaties. But residence permits, and their equivalent in Guernsey and Jersey, can be hard to get, and a level of taxpaying capacity may be required as a quid pro quo.

Switzerland is a low-tax country only in a very limited sense. The rates of tax vary considerably from one Canton to another, but nowhere does the rate payable by a resident individual come down to tax-haven levels. Nonetheless Switzerland has a lot of resident foreigners, and practices and procedures are well established: the professional advisers of an intending resident are able to discuss his position with the Cantonal tax authorities and obtain a ruling before he arrives. It is understood that they are also able to do a little discreet shopping around between Cantons, and eliminate less co-operative ones. Residence permits can, however, be difficult to obtain, especially in the more popular Cantons. There is more of a welcome for the over-sixties, so long as they do not intend to work, and they can often negotiate a lump-sum annual payment of tax (the *forfait fiscale*). A sympathetic ear is also given to individuals who make a significant investment in new industry in Switzerland.

But the individual looking for a new place of residence should not limit his horizons to the countries listed in Appendix 1. Even the United States, whose system could hardly be more unwelcoming, may merit consideration. It is not a jurisdiction in which to take up residence without careful thought and planning. The tax cost of becoming resident there has now fallen dramatically: from 1 January 1982, the maximum rate of Federal income tax is 50 per cent, and if the individual takes up residence in a 'tax-haven state' – Florida, for example – it is the limit of his liability to local tax. On the assumption that the individual makes appropriate dispositions of his income-bearing assets before becoming resident, and taking into account the 'sheltering' possibilities of municipal bonds and other forms of investment, as well as the tax credits available on non-U.S. income, the actual tax payable may be lower than is generally supposed. The unlimited marital deduction for estate tax purposes means that a man may leave all his assets to his widow, and, provided she has not become a U.S. citizen, she may in effect solve their joint estate tax problem by ceasing to reside in the United States after her husband's death.

Canada may also be considered. It gives a new resident a 'stepped-up' basis for capital gains purposes, that is his gain taxable in Canada is limited to the difference between the disposal price of the asset and its value at the date of immigration,[5] and the Canadian provisions attributing the income of offshore trusts to Canadian resident settlers do not apply to a new resident for his first five years. Except in the Province of Quebec, there are no death or succession taxes in Canada.

In Europe, the United Kingdom has a particularly advantageous fiscal regime for individuals who are resident but not domiciled there (see Chapter 3). Continental European countries generally (not Germany) seem in practice to permit a new resident to leave a substantial part of his assets in some offshore company or trust, and do not attempt to bring such assets, or their income or gains, within the local tax net, so long as the individual receives and pays tax on a reasonable income in the country and (preferably) creates some employment for others.

Temporary Emigration

A change of residence need not be permanent. In some cases, an individual may reap substantial tax benefits from changing his residence for a limited period – during which he may receive items of income, or realise capital gains or make gifts or other dispositions of his assets, any one or more of which events would have given rise to a liability to tax if he had remained resident in his original jurisdiction of residence.

A saving of tax on income generally involves making an accurate forecast of the period when the items of income in question will be received (or fall due, as the case may be). This may be possible, for example where a commission is to be payable on the happening of some future event. But it is not always necessary, for some income is not taxable until a period after that in which it is received. It is a feature of the law of the United Kingdom – a feature to be found also in a number of colonial and formerly colonial territories – that certain types of income are, as the phrase is, assessed on a preceding-year basis – that is to say, the income of the present year (1983/84) is quantified by reference to the income which accrued to the taxpayer last year (1982/83). A person carrying on a business or profession is assessed in 1983/84 on the profits which are shown in his profit and loss account for the twelve-month period ending in 1982/83; so if he makes up his accounts to, say, the end of July, he is paying tax in 1983/84 on money which he received (or earned) in the twelve months from 1 August 1981 to 31 July 1982. If he were non-resident in this tax year, while still continuing his business or profession, then the income which would fall out of charge to tax is the income which he earned during the twelve months ending in July 1982. In these circumstances, a change of residence has a retroactive effect.

In order to achieve this effect, it is not necessary that the taxpayer pass his year of absence in Monte Carlo or the Bahamas; it is sufficient that he reside in any country which does not tax such income on a previous-year basis.[6] Putting this example into general terms, an individual who moves out of a system similar to that of the United Kingdom, where tax is chargeable on certain income by reference to income earned in, or in a period which ends in, the previous fiscal year, and takes up residence in a country where tax is chargable on an actual basis, may avoid what would otherwise be a tax liability in his old jurisdiction on income arising in a period before he left, but have an exposure to tax in his new jurisdiction only on the income which arises while he is there.[7] At the same time, one should not forget that the opposite phenomenon can occur: an individual moving from an actual basis to a previous-year basis may find that his income in a certain period suffers tax in both countries.

Whereas it can in practice be difficult to time an income receipt, so that it falls into charge to tax in the period during which the taxpayer is not resident in the jurisdiction concerned, it is, by contrast, comparatively simple to organise the timing of a future capital gain. Where an asset has risen in value, and the taxpayer forms the view that the time has arrived when he should sell it, he may be quite content to postpone the sale until after the end of the current tax year, if by so doing he avoids liability to tax on the capital gain. A period of non-residence also offers the taxpayer the opportunity of increasing the base cost of his assets by means of the sale of his existing assets on the stock market, or otherwise, and the immediate repurchase of the same or similar portfolio.[8]

In some circumstances, of course, the disposal of the asset may give rise to a charge to income tax – for example, by way of recapture of writing-down allowances, or where the asset is trading stock. Here the taxpayer may examine the possibility of realising the income during a period of non-residence, and, if the income would be regarded as having its source in a high-tax country, of taking advantage of a tax treaty to obtain exemption from tax in that country.

Where the taxpayer is subject in his original jurisdiction to a tax on gifts or other dispositions, he may avoid liability to this tax by making his dispositions during a period of non-residence. The effectiveness of such a procedure depends, it goes without saying, on residence being the criterion of taxability.[9]

In general terms, a period of non-residence can offer the temporary *émigré* the opportunity of rearranging his affairs so that they are in the most appropriate form for his return to residence in his original jurisdiction, without suffering the tax cost which such rearrangement would have occasioned if he had remained resident there throughout. If in his original jurisdiction he was subject to exchange control, a period of freedom from that control may similarly afford him the opportunity lawfully to establish offshore companies or trusts whose underlying assets may be free of exchange control when he returns to his original jurisdiction.

2. Source

Since taxing jurisdictions commonly levy tax on income which has its source there,[1] regardless of the residence of the recipient, a person who by reason of his residence suffers no tax or a low rate of tax on the income will wish to ensure that the country of source imposes no tax, or no greater tax, on that income (and in the latter case that he is able to obtain credit for the source tax against the residence tax). Similar considerations apply to assets situated in another jurisdiction, where taxes are imposed on capital gains, gifts or death. Since some (though few) investments are available in zero-tax territories, and taxing jurisdictions commonly exempt certain investment income from tax in the hands of non-residents, much of the tax planning in this area is inextricably connected with investment planning. Here it is always necessary to remind oneself that what matters is the net after tax income. That the rent from a property in Monte Carlo suffers no tax is not a sufficient reason for preferring investment in a property there to, say, investment in a property in Florida. Interest on bank deposits is generally free of tax in the country of source,[2] and so is interest on Eurobonds. Governments, even in high-tax jurisdictions, commonly issue bonds whose yield, in the hands of a non-resident holder, is free of tax.

What this chapter is concerned with, however, is circumstances in which, but for tax planning considerations, the location and nature of the source would be such as to expose the owner to tax in the source country. First, consideration is given to the possibility of changing the source of the income, so that the problem does not arise in the first place. Second, consideration is given to cases where the source cannot be changed, but steps may be taken to reduce the *quantum* of income subject to tax in the source country.

Where the income arises from a trade or business, it is sometimes possible to move the profit-making apparatus to a territory which imposes either no, or a lower rate of, tax on the profits. This is an option which is available mainly to various kinds of import/export businesses and to service industries of a financial nature. But businesses involving film-making and popular music, centres of management and other expertise, and no doubt enterprises of many other characters, have been established in low-tax jurisdictions. In considering a venture of this kind, it is perhaps particularly tempting for the professional adviser to become so concerned with minimising tax on profits that he quite forgets that profits also have to be earned. This principle is perhaps best illustrated by an example.

Take an imaginary 'P. & I. Club' – that is, an association of shipowners providing mutual insurance (protection and indemnity). The administration of the Club, especially the admission or rejection of claims, and the placing of reinsurance, will be handled by professional Managers – who may also manage other Clubs. A well-managed Club will, over the years, build up a reserve – being the excess of members' contributions over claims – and this will be represented by a portfolio of investments. The Club in this example was resident in the United Kingdom. For these purposes, the United Kingdom had (and, indeed, continues to have) a number of merits: active insurance and reinsurance markets are to be found there; and the jurisdiction is not unfavourable from a tax point of view, in that the surplus arising on the mutual insurance business (that is, the excess of contributions over claims) is not treated as profit for tax purposes, because the members are not treated as making profits out of themselves. The problems arise when the surplus is invested: so long as a Club remains based in the United Kingdom the income from the investment portfolio, together with a proportion (currently 15/26ths) of the capital gains arising from disposals of the Club's investments, suffer corporation tax.[3] These were the taxes which the Club in this example sought to avoid by a move to a tax haven. Whether or not to make this move was a question which involved, in the first place, a simple cost/benefit analysis: how much tax would the Club save, and how much initial and continuing extra expense would be incurred? But the question did not quite end there, for such analysis leaves out of account the most important people involved in any operation – the customers. From the point of view of the Managers, the customers are not only the existing Club members, but possible future members: in any tax-haven operation which is not a purely private and internal one, whether it be a bond issue or the launching of a mutual fund, the important question must be, does it have customer appeal? And this is a question to be asked, of course, not only about whether or not to use a tax haven, but which tax haven to use. In this case, the Managers decided in favour of a tax haven and both the Managers and the Club moved to Bermuda.

Bermuda had the merit then, as indeed it still has, of making something of a speciality in insurance operations, especially those of the so-called 'Captive' insurance companies.[4] One can say that the Captive was an idea which was born in New York and grew up in Bermuda. Since then, the law in the United States has developed in a fashion which has restricted the uses to which a U.S.-based multinational can put a Captive. But as far as Bermuda is concerned, that development gave the Island a level of expertise in handling insurance transactions not enjoyed by any other tax haven, with the result that Bermuda acquired the reputation of being *the* place for an insurance operation. The Managers in this case chose Bermuda because the location was attractive to the members of the Club, and the reason for its attraction was not because – or at least not primarily because – the members thought Bermuda more efficient or politically more stable or geographically more convenient, but because other managers had established Clubs in Bermuda, and not to have a Club in Bermuda placed the Managers at a competitive disadvantage. From the point of view of the Managers, the purely fiscal advantages of conducting their business in Bermuda seemed, at first sight, more substantial: for them it was not merely a matter of tax on their investment income and gains (which were not significant in amount) but a question of tax on their operating profit. However, their budgets indicated that much if not all of this tax saving would be absorbed by the extra expense of conducting business in Bermuda. The cost of living on a small island tends to be significantly higher, and, while there is naturally a certain advantage in a mid-Atlantic situation for a business which has dealings in both Europe and America, it is nevertheless wise to budget for higher travelling costs. But what the Managers hoped to achieve – and subsequently succeeded in achieving – was an increase in the volume of business, which compensated them for their increased operating expenses.

Although one speaks, in general terms, of the location of a source of income, whether or not a source of income is located in a particular jurisdiction is a question to be answered in the light of the laws of that jurisdiction, and the test varies from one location to another. It may be necessary to go to considerable trouble to ensure that the business does not fall foul of the rules of other jurisdictions – for example, by conducting a complete cycle of commercial operations there, or by having an agent there, or by having title to goods pass there, or by making contracts there. So long as one is aware of the relevant pitfalls, they can, in theory, be avoided without much difficulty; what is in practice important is to do so at a tolerable cost – and here the cost can be not merely the expense of devising and administering an appropriate routine, but, if the routine cannot be fashioned so as to conform with the customers' preferred way of doing business, the cost of business lost through delay or inconvenience to the customer. In the United Kingdom, for example (and in other countries whose laws have followed the U.K. pattern), a familiar distinction is made between trading 'with' the country and trading 'in' the country – the latter, but not the former, giving rise to a tax liability. A company operating from another country, and exporting goods to customers in the United Kingdom, will seek to avoid making contracts there, or, if it has the benefit of a tax treaty, will wish to avoid having a 'permanent establishment' there.

One may, for example, consider the case of a Bahamian company engaged in the business of selling holiday homes in the Bahamas or elsewhere, which finds it necessary to conclude its contracts in the United Kingdom. This may well expose the Bahamian company to tax in the United Kingdom on the footing that it was trading there even though the customers resided elsewhere.[5] One solution to the problem would be for the Bahamian company to establish a sales company in a high-tax country which is party to a tax treaty with the United Kingdom, for example, a subsidiary in Luxembourg.[6] Such a sales company could make sales in the United Kingdom through an independent broker, and make 'back to back' purchases from the Bahamian company to cover its position. In such a structure, the Luxembourg company is exempt from U.K. tax by virtue of the U.K./Luxembourg tax treaty, since it has no 'permanent establishment' in the United Kingdom. In this particular example, however, the exemption afforded by the tax treaty is not an important feature of the structure. If the property sold by the Bahamian company to the Luxembourg company were in each case the same as that sold by the Luxembourg company to the ultimate purchaser, and the sale is made at the same time and on similar terms, there would in principle be no reason to attribute any significant profit to the Luxembourg company. If, therefore, the Luxembourg company did have a permanent establishment in the United Kingdom, its exposure to U.K. tax would be small, and such tax as it paid in the United Kingdom would be available for credit against its liability in Luxembourg. Indeed, the Bahamian company may go a step further, and establish a selling subsidiary in the very jurisdiction in which the purchasers are to be found – in this example, in the United Kingdom; for, on the principles indicated above, a relatively modest profit is all that could be attributed to it for local tax purposes.

Put in general terms, the effect of such a structure is to convert one source of income into two sources – a source wholly outside the tax reach of the high-tax jurisdictions, to which the bulk of the overall profit is attributable, and a source exposed to a high rate of tax, but whose income is of a much smaller order. International transactions of a more complex nature lend themselves, perhaps more readily, to this kind of 'fracturing' of the source. If a product is mined in country A, processed in country B with the use of know-how vested in an owner in country C, wholesaled in country D and retailed in country E, each point at which value is added may be a source of income in itself. As is well known, this phenomenon is for the international tax planner both an opportunity and a danger. Every taxing jurisdiction has some kind of 'transfer pricing' rules, which are designed to ensure that the added value taking place within that jurisdiction is reflected in the taxable profit there, and these can all too easily result in what is economically the same profit being taxable in more than one jurisdiction. Much the best approach to a problem of this kind is to ensure that each separate profit-centre makes its own genuine and independent contribution, and this is more readily made manifest where at least one entity in the chain is in separate ownership and can be shown to deal at arm's length with the entity to which the substantial profit accrues. (For a consideration of this concept in the context of the 'Stepping Stone', see pp. 71 *et seq.*)

The case of the P. & I. Club mentioned above was an example of the creation of a new source of income in substitution for an existing source in a high-tax territory. It is perhaps more common to find sources created in zero-tax or low-tax jurisdictions which have no such predecessor, and indeed this is the basis for the claim, often made by the tax havens, that international tax planning is not so much concerned with diverting taxable income into other channels, but of creating new sources of income from transactions which, but for the facilities offered by the tax havens, would not take place. This can often be seen most clearly where a joint venture is created, the venturers being resident in different countries. Typically, a Canadian, a Dutchman and a Saudi Arabian wish to go into business together; none of the parties would see any virtue in the business being established in the jurisdiction in which either of the other two resides, and they may well together form a company in the Cayman Islands which does the business there.

Reduction of Income

Where the source of income cannot be changed, it may nevertheless be possible to reduce the amount of income which is subject to the local tax. A familiar example of this is the use of local bank interest to absorb local profits. There is an almost universal rule that bank interest is payable gross to local banks and is fully deductible in computing local profits. The archetypal bank-interest transaction involves the operating company in the high-tax country borrowing from a bank in that country and paying interest which is deductible; a corresponding deposit is made by a zero-tax company in a tax haven, and the zero-tax company receives its bank interest gross and free of tax. The interest between the two banks will similarly rank as a deduction in computing the profits in the high-tax country, but it is perhaps misleading to think of such a payment taking place in isolation from the many other inter-bank transactions which will finally fall to be taken into account before any payment will actually be made. So long as bank interest can be paid out of the high-tax country without any tax liability by way of withholding or otherwise, there is no theoretical reason why the lending bank should not hold the 'back-to-back' deposit. But people often prefer to use two banks, even if the two banks are companies in the same group, and indeed the bank in the high-tax country will insist upon it if under the law of that country the right to pay interest tax-free to non-residents is limited to inter-bank interest. Non-bankers may think that this is a very easy way for a bank to make a profit, for all it is doing is lending the customer his own money. But a banker, conscious of his liquidity ratio, will not look at it like that, and the customer may expect some hard negotiation on the amount of the 'spread' between the interest paid and received. Any given spread is of course less significant in an epoch of high interest rates than it is at a time when low rates of interest are both paid and received, but the amounts to be saved with a lower spread are considerable, and some shopping around will generally be advisable.

With groups, or other related enterprises, much international tax planning is based upon the principle of taking a deduction in a high-tax jurisdiction and reaping the corresponding reward in a low-tax jurisdiction. No tax system can afford to allow such a principle to be adopted in an abusive fashion – hence the various domestic rules against artificial transfer pricing, and the various forms of withholding taxes imposed on royalties, interest, insurance premiums, management charges and other outgoings. At the same time, it is characteristic of high-tax jurisdictions that they offer various fiscal incentives, whether in their domestic law, or by way of provisions in the tax treaties to which they are party, to encourage the inflow of capital and expertise, and if there is good commercial reason for introducing these from outside, a group of related enterprises may well find it possible (perhaps by the use of a 'Stepping Stone' transaction – see pp. 71 *et seq.*) to reduce highly taxed income while increasing lowly taxed income.

Where a highly taxed enterprise can claim no relief for capital losses on long-term borrowing, it will find it fiscally advantageous to borrow the currency which is most expensive in terms of interest. More sophisticated forms of income reduction occur in the field of leasing. Tax depreciation allowances are generally available, in the case of an operating lease (that is, one covering only part of the life of the asset) to the lessor, and in the case of a financial lease (that is, one covering the whole or most of the asset's life) to the lessee, though this is not a universal rule. 'Double dipping' occurs where the lessor and lessee are in different jurisdictions, and the lessor gets a tax allowance in his country while the lessee gets a tax allowance in his. Belgium, France, Switzerland, Italy and to some extent Denmark and the United Kingdom grant allowances to lessors, and in the United States, Canada, Germany and the Netherlands, allowances may be available to the lessee. Rules vary from country to country; they have been subject to many changes in recent years and will no doubt continue to be so. Examples of double dipping have included U.S. companies leasing to the Netherlands, Swiss companies leasing in Germany and Japanese companies leasing into Brazil (where advantage results from the tax-sparing credits of the tax treaty). Where a financier provides part of the acquisition cost of the asset on a non-recourse basis, but the lessor can nevertheless claim tax allowances on 100 per cent of the cost, the fiscal advantage will accordingly be larger.

3. The United Kingdom

This and the next two chapters consider the salient features of the jurisdictions with which a practitioner in the field of international tax planning may expect to be concerned. The United Kingdom is a convenient and interesting starting point. On the one hand, it is a country whose rates of tax undoubtedly place it in the category of a high-tax jurisdiction;[1] it has a relatively high level of tax morality, and its taxation authorities, although inevitably occasioning a good deal of criticism from taxpayers, administer the system with a high level of efficiency and fairness. On the other hand, the United Kingdom – especially the City of London – has historically been, and to a large degree remains, a centre of international business, and the tax system has necessarily been required to allow persons who are not resident or not domiciled within the United Kingdom to conduct a large number of activities in the jurisdiction without suffering any local tax. Interest on many types of government security are free of tax in the hands of non-residents, and so also, in effect, is interest paid by U.K. banks; non-residents are not in general subject to capital gains tax;[2] a specially favourable regime applies to persons resident but not domiciled in any part of the United Kingdom (see below). This chapter considers the facilities which the United Kingdom makes available to those who reside or are domiciled outside its boundaries.

Non-resident Companies

The United Kingdom system treats a company as resident where it is 'managed and controlled', and this, in the ordinary case, means where the members of the board hold their meetings.[3] If by this test a company is resident in the United Kingdom, then it is liable to tax on its world income; if it is not, then its liability to tax is limited to income whose source is in the United Kingdom,[4] and as a non-resident it is generally exempt from U.K. capital gains tax.[5] The residence of a company is not determined by its place of incorporation: a company established, for example, under the law of Bermuda could, by holding its board meetings in London, have its 'management and control' in the United Kingdom, and accordingly be fully liable to corporation tax on its income and capital gains. The opposite is equally possible: a company may be incorporated in some part of the United Kingdom, yet, provided its true management and control can be shown to be outside the United Kingdom, it will be as free from tax as any corporation established in a conventional tax haven.

Strictly, the residence of the shareholders is not a material factor in determining where the control and management of a company lie, for the 'control' here in question is not that of its members in general meeting, but that of the executive officers who control and manage the conduct of its business. In practice, however, while the Inland Revenue has no objection to non-residents utilising non-resident companies to receive foreign income, there can be no question of such companies being used by residents as a means of avoiding United Kingdom tax. If the Revenue is satisfied that the true owners of the company are resident outside the United Kingdom, it will be inclined to accept its non-resident status on the basis of a statement to that effect by the lawyer or accountant acting for the company in the United Kingdom. In considering the question of ownership, the Revenue will look through any holding companies or trusts, and if the Inspector concludes that the benefit of the company's activities accrues to a company or individual resident in the United Kingdom, he is likely to make an assessment to tax on the footing that the company resides in the United Kingdom, and allow the executive officers to suffer the rigours of cross-examination at the appeal. Let it be assumed therefore for the purposes of the remainder of this part of this chapter that the person 'behind' the company is not resident in the United Kingdom.

A company may be formed in England and Wales or in Scotland or in Northern Ireland. As may be expected, the original constitution of the company (the 'memorandum and articles') and any subsequent amendments must be filed in the appropriate register.

The company must maintain a 'registered office' in the jurisdiction concerned: it is here that service of legal proceedings may be effected, and it is here that the local Inspector will direct his enquiries in the first instance. If the Inspector is satisfied that the company is non-resident and that it has no taxable U.K. income he will require no particulars of its income or assets but will enquire every two or three years, to discover whether the position is still the same. Perhaps it should be said that there is no question of the public having access to the information provided to the Inland Revenue, though taxpayers in the countries with which the United Kingdom has a tax treaty should bear in mind the provisions for exchange of information between tax authorities.[6] No permission or approval is required for the formation of a company in the United Kingdom or for the issue of shares to residents or nationals of other countries or their nominees,[7] and such formation or issue can be done with reasonable speed.

The principles on which a company incorporated in the United Kingdom may stay outside the charge to United Kingdom tax are extremely easily stated. As a practical matter, a Panamanian company (which like any other company depends for its immunity from U.K. taxation on its 'management and control' being overseas) may reasonably consider that the tax authorities in the United Kingdom have no way of making enquiries as to the places and frequency of its board meetings; a company incorporated in the United Kingdom on the other hand should at all times be in a position to demonstrate that its management and control is exercised outside the United Kingdom and for this purpose should be scrupulous to hold board meetings and keep full minutes of them. Although it is not strictly necessary, it is desirable for a company which wishes to claim not to be resident in the United Kingdom to be able to show that it is resident in some other jurisdiction; a 'gypsy' company would carry little conviction with the revenue authorities, and for this reason meetings of the directors should preferably – with perhaps the occasional exception – consistently be held in the same place. This, of course, should not be a place which itself imposes tax by reference to management and control. It is the practice for non-resident companies to keep their seal and the originals of the minutes of meetings of the board (though not of annual general meetings) outside the United Kingdom.

In January 1981, the Inland Revenue issued a consultative

paper in which it was proposed that the 'control and management' test should be replaced or augmented by a 'place of management' test. Changes in the law are not now contemplated, but a statement of practice is expected. At least until the revenue's attitude is clarified, a company claiming non-residence should be in a position to show that the place from which the management of its business as a whole is conducted is outside the United Kingdom,[8] and it may be prudent, in anticipation of a new rule of this kind, for boards of non-resident companies to begin now to include in their minutes items which will show a history of a place of management outside the United Kingdom.

The company will be required to make the usual statutory returns which are made by other companies incorporated in the United Kingdom. An abbreviated form of accounts must be filed – and those accounts are therefore open to inspection by the public. This does not appear in practice to constitute a serious obstacle to the use of companies incorporated in the United Kingdom, and since the Companies Act 1981 became law a small company files only an abbreviated balance sheet and a medium-sized company an abbreviated balance sheet and profit and loss account. If the amount of information to be made available to the public is unacceptable to the owners, they may wish to consider forming an unlimited company instead of a limited company; this involves omitting the word 'Limited' from the name of the company, but it will not expose individual owners to unlimited liability, if the shares in the unlimited company are owned by a limited company – which may be incorporated in a jurisdiction outside the United Kingdom. Shares in limited or unlimited companies may be held by nominees or trustees (a minimum of two registered shareholders are required) but nominees or trustees are unlikely in practice to be willing to hold shares in unlimited companies.

It is usual to interpose a true tax-haven company between an individual and any shareholding in a company incorporated in the United Kingdom, for the most serious drawback in the use of the United Kingdom as a place of incorporation is that shares in a United Kingdom company are property situated in the United Kingdom for capital transfer tax purposes. Individual shareholders, even though not domiciled in any part of the United Kingdom, are nevertheless liable to capital transfer tax on any gift of the shares or on any passing of the shares on their death.

This problem is best overcome by causing the shares in the United Kingdom company to be held, not by the individuals themselves, but by a company incorporated in a jurisdiction which imposes no capital tax of this kind.[9]

As indicated already, a non-resident company becomes liable to tax in the United Kingdom if it has a source of taxable income in the United Kingdom. Trading income has its source where the trade is carried on. Where a trade is carried on is a question of fact, and an important fact is where the contracts are made. Again, a degree of scrupulousness is required in the operation of a company incorporated in the United Kingdom and it is always prudent for such a company to maintain such records as will enable it to demonstrate, if challenged, that the trade has been carried on outside the United Kingdom.

The popularity of the non-resident company incorporated in some part of the United Kingdom is a phenomenon of comparatively recent origin, and its popularity has been much increased by the suspension of exchange control in October 1979 (which has made it possible for a U.K. company to have what are in effect bearer shares), and the coming into effect of the Companies Act 1981, which has made it possible for a limited company to redeem its ordinary shares. It may be that the British Government will come under pressure from its Common Market partners to curb the use of non-resident companies, or even that the Inland Revenue will persuade a Chancellor of the Exchequer that it is undesirable to have a tax-exempt entity which to the public is indistinguishable from a tax-paying one. At present, however, their existence appears to be tolerated if not encouraged, and there are no indications that any change is imminent.

The costs involved in establishing and maintaining a company in the United Kingdom compare favourably with those of other jurisdictions. In making comparisons, one should bear in mind that in the United Kingdom a company's accounts require audit, and (following the practice in other E.E.C. countries) a 1 per cent capital duty is charged on the issue of shares in limited companies.

Trusts

What is stated above about the United Kingdom as a base for companies may be regarded as well-trodden ground. Much less well known are the opportunities which the United Kingdom offers for the establishment of trusts. This is hardly surprising, for the trustees of a settlement may be liable to any one or more of three kinds of tax in the United Kingdom – income tax, capital gains tax and capital transfer tax. Where the trustees or any of them are resident in the United Kingdom, they are in principle liable to income tax[10] on the whole of the trust income, wherever arising, regardless of the residence of the beneficiaries. The exception to this rule is the kind of trust one may call an 'Interest in Possession' trust, that is where the beneficiary is entitled as of right to the trust income as it arises. In such a case, the trust is treated, in effect, as fiscally transparent: the beneficiary is regarded as the owner for the time being of the trust assets, and the income which those assets yield as his income. For example, a trust fund may be held on trust to pay the income to A for life, and subject thereto for B. During the lifetime of A (the 'life tenant'), he is to be treated as the owner of the trust assets, and the income yielded by them treated as his income. If in such a case the life tenant is not resident in the United Kingdom, and the assets are situated outside the United Kingdom, no liability to U.K. tax arises on the income, notwithstanding that the trustees are resident in the United Kingdom – though, as a precautionary measure, it is usual for the trustees to cause the income to be paid direct to the beneficiary.

For capital gains tax, the trustees are treated as being a single and continuing body of persons (distinct from persons who may from time to time be the trustees). This means that the transfer of trust property from one trustee to another – for example, on the appointment or retirement of a trustee – does not constitute any disposal or acquisition for capital gains tax purposes: the trust property remains in the hands of the notional 'continuing body'. The United Kingdom does not in general impose capital gains tax on persons who are not resident nor ordinarily resident in the United Kingdom. It is therefore very important to know where this notional body is resident, and, since none of the ordinary tests of residence can be applied to an entity which has no real existence, special rules are provided for determining the residence of trustees for capital gains tax purposes.[11] The notional body of persons is to be treated as being resident and ordinarily resident in the United Kingdom, unless the general administration of the trust is ordinarily carried on outside the United Kingdom, and the trustees – or a majority of them for the time being – are not resident or not ordinarily resident in the United Kingdom. This rule is subject to an important qualification: that a 'professional trustee', that is one who is carrying on business as such, will be treated as non-resident in relation to a particular trust so long as the settlor of that trust is neither domiciled nor resident nor ordinarily resident in the United Kingdom. There is a long tradition of major institutions in the United Kingdom accepting trust business from overseas clients, and no doubt this qualification was introduced for the express purpose of enabling that business to continue, and it seems clear that the use of U.K. trust corporations or other 'professional' trustees by settlors ordinarily resident and domiciled abroad, far from taking advantage of any anomaly in the law, is in precise conformity with Government policy in this regard.

Capital transfer tax is an amalgam of a gift tax and an estate tax. It is not levied on individuals who are domiciled outside the United Kingdom, except to the extent that they have assets which are situated in the United Kingdom. A corresponding regime is applied to trust funds, which are only liable to capital transfer tax if either the settlor was domiciled in the United Kingdom at the time when he made the settlement, or the trust assets are situated in the United Kingdom.

Trust Income: Non-Resident or Non-Domiciled Trustees

It follows from what has been said above about income tax that, where it is intended that a trust fund shall include income-bearing assets, the settlor will not, as a general rule, wish to establish his trust in the United Kingdom. To this rule, however, there are some exceptions.

Let us first consider the case where the trustee is a company incorporated within, but resident outside, the United Kingdom, in the manner described in the earlier part of this chapter. A non-resident company is free of U.K. tax on its foreign income, whether it receives the income for its own account or in a fiduciary capacity. If the function of the trust is to make investments, there is perhaps little advantage in having as trustee a company incorporated in the United Kingdom. But if the trust is to conduct a business, an English- or Scottish-incorporated company may be more welcome to a customer or business partner than a company incorporated in a tax haven. It is not altogether unknown for the trust instrument to confer on the trustee powers to carry on a trade. As a purely drafting matter, powers may be written into a trust instrument which are quite as wide as those which a corporation can exercise for its own benefit, so that whatever is required – whether to lend money or license patents or buy and sell commodities – can as well be done through a trust as through a company. The power to carry on business is not usually found in an *inter vivos* settlement; but it is common to make such a provision in drawing the will of a sole trader; and it may be that practitioners in the United Kingdom discovered the purely domestic tax advantages of the 'trading trust' as an accidental consequence of dealing with the tax affairs of will trustees.

In a case where a settlor contemplates the establishment of a trust in a zero-tax jurisdiction, with a view to the trustee forming a non-resident United Kingdom company to carry on a trade, there may be a case for considering the rather simpler alternative of appointing the non-resident company the trustee, the company carrying on the trade in its capacity as such. However, a separate company would no doubt require to be incorporated for the purpose, at any rate where the trade involves (as it generally will) the risk of liabilities which a company doing other business would be unwilling to shoulder. Like any other company incorporated in the United Kingdom, the trust company would have to file accounts, but it will not include in its balance sheet and profit and loss account the assets and income which it holds and receives in a fiduciary capacity.

The use of trusts whose trustees are companies incorporated in but resident outside the United Kingdom is an area which seems to have been little explored. Even less explored are the uses of trusts where the trustee is a company resident in the United Kingdom but incorporated elsewhere. The income of companies is as a rule liable to corporation tax, but there is an exception to that rule and that is that income received by a company in a fiduciary capacity is not liable to corporation tax but to income tax.[12] The main reason why this exception is an advantage is that the rules relating to income tax still contain the concept of 'remittance basis'. The United Kingdom taxes the overseas income of persons resident there but domiciled elsewhere only insofar as the income is remitted to the United Kingdom. A company is regarded as domiciled where it is incorporated. It follows that where a company incorporated for example in the Cayman Islands but resident in England receives as trustee income having a source outside the United Kingdom, such income is taxable on a remittance basis only.[13] In such a case, a Cayman company, with its management and control in the United Kingdom, is for all practical purposes free of United Kingdom tax. But is this any more than a clever trick, like putting one's head inside a lion's mouth? If the purpose of the structure is to avoid all liability to U.K. taxes, why not leave the management and control of the Cayman company in the Cayman Islands and simply give the United Kingdom a wide berth? Of course, it does not in general make sense to suffer the exposure to a high-tax regime, with its pitfalls on every side, unless there is some really serious benefit to go for. There are two possible benefits to be derived from having the management and control in the United Kingdom. The first is the practical one, that the management of the investments may be more expeditiously carried on in London than in the Caribbean. One may consider the case where foreign copyrights are included in the trust fund: negotiations for their exploitation may require a degree of expertise not necessarily to be found in less developed parts of the world.

The other advantage here is the benefit of the tax treaties to which the United Kingdom is a party. The trustee is a 'resident of the United Kingdom' for treaty purposes; and although the income is received by the trustee in a fiduciary capacity, it is treated, as already mentioned, as the trustee's income for tax purposes. Whether any benefit is to be gained under a tax treaty depends upon the terms of the treaty in the particular case. A straightforward example is to be found in the treaty with Hungary. Article 12 provides that royalties arising in Hungary which are paid to a resident of the United Kingdom shall be taxable only in the United Kingdom.

Frequently, however, the exemption or relief from foreign tax is expressed to be conditional upon the U.K. resident being subject to tax in respect thereof, and such treaties also provide that where the taxpayer is subject to tax on a remittance basis he is not to have relief for unremitted income. There is a condition to this effect in the French treaty,[14] and accordingly this structure would not be appropriate for royalties arising in France. Again, treaties sometimes require that income is to be 'beneficially owned' by the recipient. A trustee is not the beneficial owner of trust income. There is such a requirement in for example the Irish treaty,[15] and this structure would not, therefore be appropriate for royalties arising in the Republic of Ireland.

The exemption from tax which the treaties accord to trading profits (in the absence of a permanent establishment in the foreign country) is not generally conditional upon the taxpayer being subject to tax in respect thereof in the United Kingdom, so that this structure would be appropriate for a case where the trustees were in receipt of foreign trading income, on which they are subject to tax in the United Kingdom only on a remittance basis. Here it must be remembered that the remittance basis is limited to income which has its source outside the United Kingdom, and trading income has its source where the trade is carried on. This structure is only useful, then, where the trade is carried on wholly outside the United Kingdom. Where the United Kingdom resident is a sole trader, it will be an extremely rare case where he can show that his trade is carried on wholly outside the United Kingdom, but where he is carrying on business in partnership with a non-resident, it may not be difficult in practice to show that the whole of the partnership business is conducted outside the United Kingdom. The partnership agreement should contain an express provision – and this provision must be adhered to in practice – that the partnership business is to be managed and controlled wholly outside the United Kingdom. In those circumstances, the partnership itself will not be regarded as resident in the United Kingdom, the resident (but non-domiciled) partner will be liable to income tax on his share of the trading profits (and to capital gains tax on his share of any capital gains) only on the remittance basis. In such circumstances, also, the goodwill of the business will be located outside the United Kingdom: there need be no difficulty in keeping the cash and the goods and other assets of the business outside the United Kingdom, so that (provided the settlor was domiciled abroad) the business assets will be unaffected by capital transfer tax. Such a trust may do business (without a permanent establishment, that is) in all the countries which have concluded tax treaties with the United Kingdom and may have certain other kinds of income arising in certain of them, without any liability to tax either in the United Kingdom or in the country where the income arises.

Trust Income: Resident and Domiciled Trustees

Are there any circumstances in which it is advantageous to have as the trustee a company both resident and incorporated in the United Kingdom? Such circumstances do not arise very often in practice, but there appear to be two classes of cases where the use of a company resident and domiciled in the United Kingdom may be contemplated. The first class of case is one where a tax burden of 45 per cent is acceptable. There may, for example, be a business which has a permanent establishment in the U.K. and which finds it cheaper to pay income tax at 45 per cent than corporation tax. This is a complicated topic, for a company's corporation tax rate does not reach 45 per cent until the profits for the year reach £166,667. Moreover, the effect of treaty relief for advance corporation tax can be to reduce the net corporation tax rate below the income tax rate[16] and – since income tax is in principle leviable not on current profits but on those of a previous period – there are cash-flow considerations as well.

The second class of case where it may be advantageous to have as trustee a company resident and domiciled in the United Kingdom covers those where the previous-year basis of income tax gives the trading trust a significant lower tax charge than that of a simple trading company. There is the so-called '*cessation coup*' – perhaps more properly described as a '*commencement coup*' – which is possible under the income tax, but not under the corporation tax, rules. To put the concept[17] in a nutshell: the general rule is that income tax is levied each fiscal year on the trading profits shown in the accounts ending in the previous fiscal year; this (logically) calls for special rules to deal with the fiscal years when the trade is just beginning (where there is no account ending in a previous fiscal year) and to deal with the accounting periods prior to the cessation of the trade (which would otherwise be linked to fiscal years in which no trade is carried on and therefore contain no source of income capable of being taxed). These special rules work rather arbitrarily either in favour of the taxpayer or in favour of the Revenue, depending on the profit pattern in the particular case; the secret of the *coup* lies in programming the profits over a four- or five-year period, and if this is done successfully (and the rules are not changed during the period) the effective tax rate on the profits of the trading trust may be halved.

The other circumstance in which the 'previous-year basis' for income tax merits some close attention is where there is a trust which is resident in the United Kingdom in one fiscal year but not resident in the next. Suppose there is in prospect a large single transaction which needs the protection of a tax treaty to prevent the trading profit from being taxed elsewhere – in the absence, that is, of a permanent establishment in the other country. Suppose the trust has been trading for some time and that the trustee is resident in the United Kingdom in the year in which the large profit arises, but not resident in the United Kingdom in the fiscal year in which the tax would be payable. Let it also be assumed that the trade continues despite the change of residence, so that the effect of such a series of events is intended to be that the trust company is entitled to the benefit of the relevant tax treaty and accordingly exempt from the foreign tax on the large profit, but is not required to pay any U.K. tax because of its change of residence. In this context, it must be borne in mind that section 482 of the Income and Corporation Taxes Act 1970 prohibits a company resident in the United Kingdom from changing its residence without the consent of the Treasury. Such consent is unlikely to be given in a case of this kind, but fortunately there are some general consents, and a trust company formed for the purpose by non-resident shareholders could take advantage of general consent No 1.[18]

Lastly, one should mention the possibility of having a resident and domiciled trustee, in a case where the trust assets are invested outside the United Kingdom, and the life tenant or other person with an interest in possession is resident outside the United Kingdom. A variety of Interest in Possession trust is the so-called 'thin trust'. Typically, a settlor may settle assets upon trust to pay income to himself for life and subject thereto as he may by deed or will appoint, and subject thereto for his wife absolutely. The trust is 'thin' not merely because it is contained in a few pages, but because it is, so to speak, only just a trust – being closer to a nomineeship or bare trust than to the conventional type of offshore trust. Since, as already mentioned, the income of an Interest in Possession trust is treated as belonging to the life tenant as it arises,[19] there would be no liability to U.K. tax by reason of the residence or domicil of the trustee. It is doubtful whether the trustee of an Interest in Possession trust can claim any of the benefits of the tax treaties, and indeed there seems no reason in such circumstances to prefer a U.K. resident trustee over one resident elsewhere. But there can sometimes be non-fiscal reasons for preferring a U.K. trustee – for example, because the portfolio management requires to be carried on in the United Kingdom, or because exchange control consent for payments to the trustee is more readily obtainable where the trustee is a U.K. resident than where he is resident in a zero-tax jurisdiction.[20]

Trust Capital Gains

The cases where the United Kingdom is an advantageous *situs* for trust assets of an income-yielding nature may be regarded as exceptional. But where the trust assets do not, or need not, yield income, the trustee intending merely to realise a capital gain on their disposal, the use of a 'professional' trustee resident in the United Kingdom (but not treated as such for capital gains tax) may be more strongly indicated. Thus an intending settlor who is neither resident, ordinarily resident nor domiciled in the United Kingdom, minded to settle a policy of assurance, or a controlling shareholding in a company (dividends on which need not be declared), may well choose a U.K.-resident trust company as his trustee. For the reasons already mentioned, capital transfer tax considerations will require that the trust investments are confined to assets situated outside the United Kingdom, but it should not be forgotten that where trustees invest in the United Kingdom, a capital transfer tax liability can arise whether they are resident in the United Kingdom or not, and trustees (like individuals) should make their investments in the United Kingdom through the medium of a non-U.K. company.

Again, while there is no positive merit, from a tax point of view, in choosing a U.K.-resident trustee in such circumstances, there will in general be no fiscal demerit in doing so, and the advantage of appointing a U.K. trustee may be of a practical rather than a fiscal nature. However, although the trustee may be *treated* as non-resident for capital gains tax, he is nevertheless *actually* resident, and it is submitted that he ought to be entitled to take advantage of those tax treaties (e.g. the treaty with Canada)[21] which give to a U.K. resident a measure of exemption from foreign taxes on capital gains.

Non-domiciled Individuals

The concept of 'domicil' is familiar to all those brought up in the tradition of English law, but it is so alien to the concepts of civil law that it needs a brief explanation here. An individual is domiciled in a jurisdiction if he truly belongs there. An infant has his father's domicil – or his mother's if he is illegitimate – during his infancy, and retains that domicil on attaining his majority. It is his 'domicil of origin'. By going to live elsewhere with the intention of making it his permanent home, he can acquire a 'domicil of choice' in some other jurisdiction. An individual cannot be without a domicil: if circumstances giving rise to such domicil of choice cease, new circumstances may create a new domicil of choice, but if they do not, the individual's domicil of origin revives. It is inherent in the concept of domicil that an individual may live a long time in a place without becoming domiciled there. Suppose, for example, a man born and brought up in the province of Alberta decides that, after his retirement, he would like to live in London for some years; he likes living in Belgravia, and is fond of going to the theatre, but he never intends to end his days in England, having a definite plan to return to Calgary in the future. He will be a typical example of an individual resident and ordinarily resident in the United Kingdom, but not domiciled in any part of the United Kingdom.

A non-domiciled person residing in the United Kingdom pays local property taxes on his property and suffers value added tax and similar taxes on his purchases, but many a retired person, living off his investments, has taken up residence in the United Kingdom on the footing that income tax, capital gains tax and capital transfer tax are mere voluntary levies, which he may either suffer or not suffer, as he wishes. Such an individual can, of course, achieve a similar freedom from taxes by going to live in one of the zero-tax jurisdictions, but the government of any jurisdiction requires an income to meet its outgoings, and where no (or little) direct tax is levied, the government must depend to a much larger extent on indirect taxes, so that the individual from Alberta, in the above example, is likely to find that if he goes to live in the Bahamas he will make a much more substantial contribution to the maintenance of the schools and roads than he will in the United Kingdom.

Income tax and capital gains tax are levied on non-domiciled individuals resident in the United Kingdom on the 'remittance basis' referred to earlier, as regards foreign income and gains on foreign assets. The non-domiciled individual will therefore invest only outside the United Kingdom, and will organise his investment and banking so that he remits only capital and not income or capital gains. (An Interest in Possession trust (see p. 28) may be helpful in this connection.) Such investments are 'excluded property' for capital transfer tax purposes, and they may pass under his will or his intestacy or be the subject-matter of *inter vivos* gifts without attracting any capital transfer tax liability. In practice, an individual with a foreign domicil of origin can enjoy this favourable regime for income tax and capital gains tax more or less indefinitely; his immunity from capital transfer tax, however, comes to an end after seventeen years of continuous residence in the United Kingdom.[22]

4. Low-Tax Jurisdictions

The tendency in recent years has been for offshore business to move away from zero-tax jurisdictions to territories which, while imposing tax on their own residents, do so in such a way that non-residents can either be exempt or suffer tax at an acceptably low rate. This chapter considers the salient features of these territories. The scheme adopted here is not to provide a list of what is, so to speak, 'on offer', territory by territory,[1] but rather to consider, one at a time, the resulting phenomena. Those territories whose use to the international tax planner is based upon their enjoying a territorial system of taxation are considered as a group; the next group consists of those which allow a special status to non-resident companies; next comes the group of territories which offer a special exempt status to certain kinds of companies; next those whose important feature is that they combine a low rate of domestic tax with relief under tax treaties. The final sections of this chapter group together jurisdictions which are of interest to the international tax planner because they provide facilities of a particular nature – holding companies, unlimited companies, captive companies, partnerships, trusts, mutual funds, special shares, locations for 'management and control' and administrative offices, the maintenance of numbered accounts, and the ownership of land.

The Territorial Basis

An alternative to the zero-tax jurisdiction is the country which does not tax income arising outside its frontiers. These are listed under 'territorial basis' in paragraph 5, Appendix 1. They include the classic tax havens, Liberia and Panama, where incorporation is quick, easy and cheap, and which in practice function in very much the same way as the zero-tax jurisdictions.

Panama has been in the tax-haven business for a very long time. Their Companies Law, modelled on that of the state of Delaware, was enacted in 1927, and it has never been substantially changed despite the various changes of regime since that time. Companies can be formed quickly and easily; the amount of information filed on Companies' Registry is extremely small, and in particular gives no indication as to the identity of the shareholders. The Law requires no annual general meetings. No annual returns have to be filed. The variety of endings which are possible for the company name (see paragraph 13 of Appendix 1) means that one may find at a Belgian address a company whose name ends in 'Société Anonyme', or at a German address a company ending in 'Aktiengesellschaft', and a company may adopt the ending 'Limitée' for use in Canada, 'NV' for Holland or 'Inc.' for the United States. The one ending which a Panamanian company may not use is 'Ltd'; that is reserved for the limited partnership. Nor may a company have a name which suggests that it conducts a banking or reinsurance business unless it has the approval of the Banking Commission or Reinsurance Commission as the case may be, and opens a bank or reinsurance company in Panama. The approval of the Banking Commission is also required if the word 'trust' is to be employed in the name of the company.

Very similar facilities are offered by Liberia, except that the name of a Liberian corporation may end in 'Ltd'. There is a minimum capital of U.S. $500 for a Liberian corporation, but none for a Panamanian corporation. Neither country has exchange control, and in both shares may be denominated in any currency. Shares may be either issued or not, and in either nominative or bearer form, as may be desired. Every Panamanian company must have a resident agent, who must be an attorney. Panama has a territorial system of tax generally; Liberia applies a similar system to corporations more than 50 per cent of whose stock is held by non-Liberians. Neither country imposes any tax on dividends arising from operations abroad. It follows that one may use Panamanian and Liberian companies to receive and distribute income arising outside their respective frontiers.

There are three features of Panama which call for special mention. First, it has the Colon Free Zone. If an enterprise is supplying Central and South America, it may maintain a buffer stock there, or otherwise repack and reship goods destined for other countries, especially pharmaceuticals, electronics equipment and other easily transportable merchandise.[2] Secondly, if an enterprise has personnel travelling around Central and South America, Panama may be a good place to locate them. So long as they are working basically outside Panama, they may reside in Panama without being liable to income tax there, and may also enjoy certain customs duty privileges. Thirdly, Panama has become a very important banking centre for the area, and most of the major international banks are well represented there. Their bank secrecy law is tough: it appears to be directed primarily towards ensuring the confidentiality of numbered accounts – which they have in Panama, but the legislation is equally applicable to bank accounts of other kinds.

The Costa Rican tax system is a territorial one. In consequence, a Costa Rican company doing business abroad is not taxed on its income generated abroad. Shares can be denominated in a foreign currency, though they can no longer be in bearer form. Costa Rica has a mild form of exchange control: this does not preclude ownership of bank accounts in foreign countries nor the export of foreign currency abroad, but it does impose on the holder of foreign currency who wishes to sell or exchange it in Costa Rica the obligation to sell it to the State banks. This small disadvantage need not prevent a Costa Rican company which does international business from doing its banking in Costa Rica, where there is a high level of bank secrecy. Unlike Panama and Liberia, Costa Rica imposes a withholding tax on dividends, which amounts to 15 per cent on distributions to non-residents, but this may not present a problem in practice, for it is understood that the tax authorities do not pursue this liability where all the transactions relating to the distributions are carried out outside the country, and no tax is in any event chargeable on the redemption of a debenture or other repayment of a loan, and – more importantly – the tax is not chargeable on the distribution in a winding up.

The laws of Costa Rica and of Panama make provision for the establishment of trusts, but this is little used in practice, if only because it is hard to predict how the Court would resolve problems of interpretation which might arise in the course of the administration of the trust, and indeed, it would be a very remarkable draftsman who could encapsulate in a Spanish-language statute anything comparable to the rules of equity, as developed by the Courts over many years in England and in countries deriving their law from English law. But a Liberian, Panamanian or Costa Rican company may well be chosen as the operating vehicle by the trustees of a trust established elsewhere – in the Cayman Islands, for example, or in England (see pp. 29 *et seq.*). The greater advantage of Costa Rica is that it has not yet been 'discovered': the fact that a company is incorporated in Liberia or Panama suggests (rightly or wrongly) to everyone dealing with it that it owes its existence to some kind of tax planning; this is not true of a company incorporated in Costa Rica.

Hong Kong has a similar element of territoriality in its tax legislation; it has the advantage of being a great international business centre in its own right, but it has the disadvantage that the tax authorities there take a much stricter view than their opposite numbers in Costa Rica, Liberia or Panama as to what profits are to be regarded for these purposes as arising outside their jurisdiction (though since Hong Kong currently imposes tax on companies' profits at the rate of only 16½ per cent, the penalty for failing to qualify for the exemption is not a very great one). Hong Kong has no wealth tax or capital gains tax, and no withholding tax on dividends. Interest will suffer withholding tax at 15 per cent if the source of interest is in Hong Kong. Foreign currency deposits with financial institutions are exempt, however, and interest tax on Hong Kong dollar deposits with financial institutions is imposed at a reduced rate of 10 per cent. In determining the source of interest, Hong Kong looks to the place where the credit is made available to the borrower. Royalties from patents, designs, trademarks and know-how used in Hong Kong itself are deemed to have a Hong Kong source, but only 10 per cent of a royalty which has its source in Hong Kong suffers Hong Kong tax. There is a 'closely connected' rule by which transfer prices between a resident and connected non-resident may be effectively adjusted by deeming the business of the non-resident to be carried on in Hong Kong. Resident shipowners pay Hong Kong tax on shipping profits, and 'resident' for this purpose includes companies incorporated in Hong Kong. But the amount of profit chargeable to tax may be reduced by a bareboat charter to a non-resident or by interest charges or capital allowances. Where a non-resident sells goods in Hong Kong through an agent, tax may be based on a percentage of turnover. Reinvoicing and like transactions between non-residents may require the use of an agent outside Hong Kong. The Colony does, however, have estate duty, and it is therefore not generally wise for an individual to hold shares in a Hong Kong company.

The United States Virgin Islands has a kind of territorial basis in its tax system, and in recent years a number of foreign corporations have sought to take advantage of this by establishing 'residence' there. The advantage, however, is not limited to exemption from tax in the Virgin Islands, for where a resident foreign company's income has its source in the United States itself, it is exempt from tax there also.

The United States does not tax a Virgin Islands resident on any income – not even income arising in the United States. The U.S. Code has effect in the Virgin Islands, but as a separate tax system – as a 'mirror' of the U.S. Code. The revised Organic Act provides that a Virgin Islands resident satisfies all his U.S. income tax obligations by filing a return in the Virgin Islands, and has no obligation to file any return in the United States. No U.S. withholding tax is charged on dividends or other payments to a Virgin Islands resident. Revenue ruling 80/40 recognises that U.S. domestic corporations can be resident in the Virgin Islands: it seems that a foreign-incorporated company can also be resident in the Virgin Islands if, among other things, it has its management and control there. A Court will probably look at all the facts and circumstances in deciding a question of residence: a corporation wishing to be considered resident in the Virgin Islands should not only hold its directors' meetings there but should also have an active business there or some other business purpose for establishing residence in the Virgin Islands – beyond that of minimising income taxes.

Income arising to a foreign corporation from a source outside the Virgin Islands (unless 'effectively connected' with a business conducted in the Virgin Islands) is not 'income' in the Virgin Islands, by virtue of section 882 (*b*) of the U.S. Internal Revenue Code, and a foreign-incorporated company is still a 'foreign corporation' for these purposes, even if its place of incorporation is in the United States. This regime is therefore particularly attractive to companies with U.S. source-income. But where the company resident in the Virgin Islands is incorporated in some part of the United States, it may be used to receive income which has its source in other countries, obtaining, by virtue of its place of incorporation, the benefit of the tax treaties to which the

United States is party, without suffering (by virtue of its place of residence) any United States tax or (because its income has a foreign source) any tax in the Virgin Islands.

If more than 50 per cent of the income of a foreign company resident in the Virgin Islands is not effectively connected with the conduct of a trade or business in the Virgin Islands, no withholding tax is levied on its dividends. The attitude of the U.S. Internal Revenue Service to these uses of the Virgin Islands is uncertain, but it is perhaps significant that after the Foreign Investment in Real Property Taxes Act had been introduced to Congress, the Treasury saw fit to introduce an amendment for the purpose of preventing the Virgin Islands being used as a route for the avoidance of this tax.

Seychelles requires to be mentioned here because taxpaying companies there are not taxed on their foreign income, nor are dividends paid by a Seychellois company out of income arising outside Seychelles subject to any tax.

Singapore and Malaysia[3] have an element of territoriality in their tax systems. Both these countries have anti-avoidance provisions in their Income Tax Acts, one of whose effects is similar to that of the old 'surtax direction' provisions in the United Kingdom (now replaced by the present 'apportionment' provisions, restricted to investment income). These allow the Revenue to treat a company's income as distributed even though it has not in fact been distributed. It has always been the practice in the United Kingdom not to apply these provisions to companies at least 90 per cent of whose shares are held by non-residents, and a similar practice appears to be followed in Malaysia and Singapore, so that (as in Costa Rica) the dividend tax may be avoided by simply not declaring dividends, the ultimate reward to the shareholders being by way of a distribution in the winding up of the company. But this freedom from 'surtax direction' is not a publicly stated practice, and there must therefore always be some element of uncertainty in this area when a company resident in either of these countries is used for a transaction of this kind.

A company incorporated in South Africa is not liable to South African tax on its foreign-source income. Certain kinds of foreign-source income, however, would be deemed in its hands to have a South African source – notably bank interest. This immunity from tax results from the territorial nature of the South African system, and does not depend on the residence of the company, though a distinction between residents and non-residents is made in the charge to withholding tax on payments of South African source interest or royalties and on dividends paid out of South African source profits – the withholding tax being levied where the payer is a resident and not where the payer is a non-resident. But the distinction is of crucial importance when it comes to exchange control. The Republic still has a stringent system of exchange control, and a South African company – whatever its residence for tax – will be of limited usefulness unless it is treated as not resident for exchange control. It is understood that as a practical matter such treatment is more likely to be afforded to a company if it can show that its management and control are outside South Africa.

Liechtenstein[4] and Switzerland[5] fit rather awkwardly into the category of countries which tax on the territorial basis: it is true that they do not in principle tax certain kinds of foreign income – notably rents from foreign immovable property (a feature also found in the Netherlands – see pp. 49 *et seq.*); what is more important is that their domiciliary companies enjoy tax benefits as regards business income – exemption from all income tax in Liechtenstein and from Cantonal income tax in Switzerland – only if their business activities are essentially conducted abroad. But they are also examples of countries which levy a distribution tax on outgoing dividends. In Liechtenstein, this is not a serious problem: the rate is only 4 per cent, and it applies only to companies whose capital is divided into shares, and not to the *Anstalt* or establishment, which is the vehicle most commonly used. In Switzerland, by contrast, the distribution tax is very serious indeed; the rate is 35 per cent, and it cannot be avoided by accumulating income during the life of the company, because it applies also to the resulting capital distribution in a winding up. The Swiss withholding tax may be reduced to a lower or zero rate under a tax treaty, and that is why one often finds a Swiss company owned by a Dutch holding company, but this device is currently under some attack in Berne, and its future at present is a little uncertain.

Non-resident Companies

The list headed 'Non-resident Companies' in paragraph 4 of Appendix 1 shows the territories which follow the United Kingdom rule of not imposing any tax on the income of a company which is incorporated there, provided it is not resident there – that is, provided its 'management and control' can be shown to be somewhere else. This is the principle behind the well-known 'corporation tax' companies in Guernsey and Jersey, and their equivalent in the Isle of Man. Less well known in this context are the British Virgin Islands, and a few words about this remarkable Colony may therefore be appropriate here. The British Virgin Islands, a few miles away from the United States Virgin Islands, are in marked contrast quiet and somnolent and have no discernible crime. Though less wealthy than the United States Virgin Islands, they have what is by Caribbean standards a high *per capita* income; they have virtually no poverty, and they enjoy extremely low personal and company taxes.[6] Unlike the population of the United States Virgin Islands, with its mix of blacks, Danes, Latin Americans and (for the most part transient) continental Americans, that of the British Virgin Islands is overwhelmingly black. The Islands are extravagantly pretty, and remarkably free from social stress; indeed, the people there lead what seems to the outsider a life bordering on the idyllic. Until recently, investors were able to use companies in the British Virgin Islands to obtain the benefit of the old tax treaty between the United Kingdom and the United States. This extension of the treaty has now, however, come to an end, and attempts to make a new treaty appear to have foundered. So the main interest of the British Virgin Islands today lies in the use of their non-resident companies.

The governments of all these territories – the British Virgin Islands, Guernsey, the Isle of Man and Jersey – levy (unlike the United Kingdom) a fixed annual tax on non-resident companies incorporated there. This tax has become an important source of revenue for these islands, and it is perhaps therefore not surprising that, so long as a company pays this tax without delay, the tax authorities may be found to be disinclined to enquire too closely, whether or not the true management and control of the company takes place where the boards meetings are held.

Israel treats a company as non-resident for tax purposes if (*a*) its management and control and (*b*) its principal activity are outside the country. It is understood that a designation as non-resident for exchange control is more easily obtained if the company either agrees to pay tax at a low rate (5–7 per cent) or passes its receipts through an Israeli bank.

The same rule applies in St Vincent; although the laws of that territory provide specific exemptions from local tax for resident companies doing international business. The exemption is subject to conditions and obtainable only on payment of a fee, and neither the conditions nor the fee apply to a company which is merely incorporated in St Vincent but not resident there.

Exemptions

In paragraph 2 of Appendix 1 is a list of jurisdictions which provide express exemptions for companies doing international business. St Vincent is included for the reason mentioned above, and Grenada because it still has a rather simpler kind of international business company legislation of the sort which began in Jamaica and was adopted by Barbados – giving complete exemption to foreign trading income, but imposing a 2½ per cent tax on foreign investment income. This legislation is no longer in force in Jamaica, but it still exists in Barbados, where it has been recently amended so as to impose a small tax on trading income as well. The new Companies Act (1982-84) revises and reforms the company law of Barbados:[7] it permits incorporation by a single shareholder, abolishes the *ultra vires* doctrine, permits companies (if solvent) to buy their own shares, requires only one director (unless the company is a public company), and exempts small companies from the necessity of audit.

Two types of companies resident in the Isle of Man may enjoy effective exemption from local tax. (This is quite separate from the exemption enjoyed by non-resident companies – see p. 46.) The Exempt Insurance Companies Act 1981 makes provision for exemption to be granted to an insurance company the whole of whose underwriting risks are located outside the Isle of Man. The Manx Government imposes certain conditions, as a prerequisite to the grant of the necessary licence and of exempt status – conditions designed to ensure that companies operating under this regime are solvent and well run. The other type of company which may be effectively exempt from Manx tax is the resident investment company. Such a company, may, by concession, pay dividends to non-residents free of withholding tax. Since dividends are deductible in computing the profits of Manx resident companies for tax purposes, it follows that where an investment company distributes the whole of its income to non-residents, and no withholding tax is charged on the distributions, no liability for Manx tax arises. A similar effect may be achieved by the use of a unit trust, but this results from the quite different principle that, where a trust is funded from sources outside the Isle of Man, has no income from sources in the Isle of Man (other than bank interest) and has its beneficiaries resident outside the Isle of Man, the trust is, by concession, not assessed to Manx tax (see p. 82).

Cyprus is included because of its exemption for shipping companies and for partnerships of non-residents and branches of non-resident companies engaged in offshore activities.[8] Djibouti is a newcomer to the tax-haven business: it now offers a tax-exempt status to companies established in its tax-free zone. Gibraltar is included because of its Exempt Company,[9] Israel because it grants a special exemption to International Trading Companies, and Seychelles because of its little-known 'Exempt Entity'. This enjoys exemptions which cover stamp duties as well as tax, and any exchange control would not apply to an Exempt Entity. No audited accounts are required by statute. No-par value shares and bearer shares are permitted. There is a provision for change of domicil: a foreign company may transfer its domicil to Seychelles, and a Seychellois Exempt Entity may transfer its domicil elsewhere[10] and buy in its own shares.

Denmark is included in this list because of its foundations and its co-operatives. The use of Danish foundations by non-residents is uncommon, but they seem worth exploring. These institutions are used in Denmark to meet purely domestic requirements. The family foundation is created by a donor to benefit others. He himself cannot benefit, but he may join the board of the foundation. What is interesting about this institution from a tax point of view is that the only income of a foundation which is taxed is that derived from business activities: no tax is levied on investment income, nor is any tax charged on the establishment of the foundation or on the distribution of funds to beneficiaries, so that beneficiaries resident outside Denmark suffer no Danish tax.

The co-operative is a common feature of economic life in

Denmark. Such a body is taxed not on its actual income but on a notional income proportionate to its capital, the annual tax liability being less than 1 per cent of the capital. There seems nothing to prevent persons resident outside Denmark from forming a Danish co-operative and becoming entitled in that capacity to benefit from the tax treaties to which Denmark is party. No tax is levied on dividends or on proceeds of winding up paid to members who are resident outside Denmark. The establishment of a co-operative society requires no permission and no registration. It is constituted by an agreement between the parties. The agreement must provide for a General Meeting and each member must have one – and only one – vote, but otherwise the agreement may provide whatever the parties wish, including limited liability. To obtain the favourable tax treatment for the society, however, the agreement must provide for the profits to be distributed to the members in proportion to the business each member does with the society.

Two very recent newcomers to this list are Antigua and the Cook Islands. Until 1982, Antigua had the old Jamaica-style International Business Companies Act (p. 47) but the new legislation provides for complete tax exemption for corporations doing international business. The Antiguan Act is in detail very different from that of the Cook Islands, but its effect is substantially similar (though permitting the use of foreign words or abbreviation to indicate limited liability). The Cook Islands company law (of 1982) provides a complete exemption from taxes and duties to companies which do business only with persons resident elsewhere. The legislation is extremely well thought out, and contains a number of desirable features – permitting international companies to have bearer shares and shares of no-par value and to transfer their domicil to any other jurisdiction with similar provisions in its legislation (see Note 10). Licences are required for banking or insurance business.

The name of the company must end in one of the prescribed ways: the last word may be Limited or Ltd, Incorporated or Inc., or simply Corporation or Corp.

Low-tax Companies with Treaty Relief

The Netherlands appears in three of the paragraphs of Appendix 1 – in paragraph 3 (countries suitable for a holding company), in paragraph 6 (low-tax countries with treaty relief) and in paragraph 5 (countries which tax on a territorial basis). This country features in paragraphs 3 and 6 for the same reason – because of the 'participation privilege'. In general, one finds in the Netherlands everything which is the antithesis of a tax haven: the Dutch tax administration is both sophisticated and strict, and the tax rates in Holland are high. At the same time, the Netherlands has a long history of involvement in international business and one may expect the tax inspector to be willing to facilitate international transactions. Perhaps the commonest use of the Netherlands in international transactions is its use as a location for a holding company. The fundamental concept here is what the Dutch call a 'qualifying participation'. A qualifying participation, in general terms, is a holding in a company which is subject to tax (at whatever rate) in some country, where the holding involves some active participation in the affairs of the company and is not a mere passive investment. The requisite holding is, in law, a mere 5 per cent, but it is understood that in practice the Dutch tax authorities may be unwilling to treat a holding of less than 50 per cent, as involving 'active participation'. No Dutch tax is charged on dividends or capital gains arising from a qualifying participation; equally, expenses relating to a qualifying participation are not deductible.

It follows that an ordinary Netherlands company which has a qualifying participation in a foreign company can receive and accumulate dividends, without, in theory, any Dutch tax becoming payable on the dividends. But the company will generally wish to obtain from the tax authorities a ruling that a proposed investment will qualify, and this will sometimes be given on the footing that a small amount of Dutch tax is paid. A Netherlands company is subject to withholding tax on its dividends, and for this reason its shares are often held by a Netherlands Antilles company – income flowing tax-free from Holland to the Antilles, and the Antilles company paying tax there at the reduced rate of 2½ to 3 per cent. Since the Antilles does not impose withholding taxes, no tax charge arises on the distribution of dividends.

Although the Netherlands appears in paragraph 5 of Appendix 1 (countries with a territorial basis), its system of tax is not truly territorial like that of Costa Rica or Panama. But certain forms of foreign income are excluded from the tax base – without being excluded in determining the rate of tax chargeable – and, in consequence, a Netherlands company does not pay Dutch tax on the profits of a foreign branch, so long as the jurisdiction where the branch is established either is a treaty country or imposes tax on the profits.

The Netherlands Antilles is listed in paragraph 6: it was perhaps the earliest territory to offer a combination of low tax and treaty relief, and although these advantages have been somewhat eroded, as regards the U.S. and U.K. treaties, they are still very important. Tax rates are high and tax is effectively administered. But lower rates are applicable to most offshore transactions. Thus, dividends and interest on securities, rents from real property and patent royalties suffer tax at a rate of 2.4 to 3 per cent; capital gains are not taxed. Reasonable expenses are deductible, and there are no withholding taxes. Companies benefiting from this regime are excluded from the U.K. and U.S. treaties; but a company may elect to pay higher rates of tax, and if it does so, it becomes entitled to the benefit of the U.K. and U.S. treaties. The higher rates are 15 per cent on dividends and 24–30 per cent on interest and royalties, but expenses are allowed in arriving at the income to be taxed at this rate, and rulings are commonly given to finance companies such as to leave only a small turn or 'spread' subject to tax. Rulings are also available which effectively provide for modest rates of tax for offshore businesses, for example, captive insurance or offshore banking.

Switzerland appears in paragraphs 2 and 3 of Appendix 1, offering a low-tax regime to certain companies (see Appendix 2), which may nevertheless obtain the benefit of the tax treaties to which Switzerland is a party.

Barbados, Grenada and St Vincent fall into this category because of their International Business Companies (p. 47), the British Virgin Islands (p. 46), because of its 15 per cent tax rate and Cyprus because of its Offshore Companies.[11] In this group also falls the Republic of Ireland: it has a new flat rate of 10 per cent corporation tax on manufacturing profits, to replace the former system of tax exemptions; income, profits and gains of other kinds are fully taxable.

In all these cases, there are possible combinations of relief under the relevant treaty from tax in the country where the income arises, whether in the form of interest or royalties or dividends or business profits or any other form, with a low-tax price in the country of receipt. These possibilities are considered in Chapter 6.

Holding Companies

Of the countries suitable for holding companies, Luxembourg is perhaps the best known – and deservedly so, for the holding company legislation has been a feature of their law since the late 1920s, and continues to be much utilised for both direct and portfolio investment. A holding company is permitted only limited activities. It may acquire, hold and sell or otherwise exploit certain investments. Shares, stocks and patents have always been permitted investments; these have recently been extended to include currencies and bullion. It may administer and control its investments from Luxembourg. But it may not, if it is to keep its tax-exempt status, run a commercial business open to the public. It may not own property, or real estate, except in order to provide itself with offices. It may not act as a broker or commission agent. Although holding companies in Luxembourg are not subject to tax on income or distributions, an annual tax is levied on their issued capital. It is at the modest rate of 0.2 per cent, and is levied on the market value of the issued shares of the company. In the case of unquoted companies, the market value of the shares is taken to be whichever is the larger of the nominal capital or an amount equal to ten times the total dividend paid in respect of the previous year, so that there is an effective tax rate of at least 2 per cent on dividends. Luxembourg holding companies are not entitled to the benefit of tax treaties to which Luxembourg is a party.

Holding companies are also free of income tax in Liechtenstein and free of Federal income tax in Switzerland (see Appendix 2) on dividends they receive, though there may in Liechtenstein and will in Switzerland be tax on outgoing dividends.

The distinguishing feature of the holding company in Nauru is the secrecy surrounding its affairs: no records are available for public inspection and any court proceedings relating to a holding company will generally be held *in camera*.

Holding companies in the Netherlands have already been discussed (see p. 50); similar rules apply in the Netherlands Antilles.

Unlimited Companies

A list of territories which permit the formation of companies whose liabilities are unlimited is set out in paragraph 7 of Appendix 1. Unlimited companies are not very often used in international tax planning, but they are useful when a parent company wants to give an offshore subsidiary what is in effect the benefit of its guarantee, and in the British jurisdictions they generally have the advantage that shares can be issued and share capital increased without liability to capital duty or stamp duty and that their share capital can be reduced without the consent of the Court. They are also useful where the company does not wish to have the word 'limited' or its equivalent in its name (a privilege which, unexpectedly, is also accorded to a limited company in Turks and Caicos and, if it is an Exempt Company, in Cayman.)[12]

Captive Companies

In paragraph 8 of Appendix 1 is a list of the territories suitable for what are there called 'Captive companies' – that is, companies which are not dealing with the public at large, but serve the interests of a multinational parent, or of a group of enterprises belonging to the same family or other limited group.[13] For banks, and trust companies there is often some kind of licensing requirement, and a requirement of minimum capitalisation; these are unlikely in practice to present insurmountable obstacles to any kind of legitimate enterprise, but a licence will always involve a licence fee, and these seem to get larger every year. Listed separately are the territories where no licence is required for a trust company.

Partnerships, Trusts and Mutual Funds

Useful jurisdictions which permit the formation of partnerships and limited partnerships are listed in paragraph 9 of Appendix 1.[14] In paragraph 10, there is a list of jurisdictions where the law permits the making of settlements. These are not quite the same countries as those listed in paragraph 8 as jurisdictions for establishing trust companies, since it is possible to have a trust company in a country which does not recognise a law of trusts.

It is not uncommon, for example, to find a settlement governed by the law of the Cayman Islands of which the trustee is a Swiss company or which is administered by a Swiss branch of a Cayman company. Also listed in paragraph 10 are jurisdictions which permit the formation of a unit trust or a mutual fund. A mutual fund is essentially an incorporated form of unit trust, and the feature required of the law, if a territory is to be suitable for mutual funds, is that it should permit a company to redeem its own shares without the consent of the Court or other formality. The Channel Islands do not permit reduction of capital as such, but the same effect may be produced by having a class of participating preference shares with a nominal value of 1p or 1 cent. These are issued and redeemed at a premium, the managers at the same time issuing to themselves an equivalent number of virtually valueless shares with the same nominal value. The authorities in the Channel Islands have recently taken to imposing somewhat strict conditions upon the establishment of new mutual funds (without apparently reviewing the conditions under which existing funds operate). While those Islands remain suitable for large funds managed by well-known financial institutions, anything in the nature of an 'in-house' fund will probably find at the present time a better welcome in the Isle of Man or in one of the other territories on this list.

Special Shares

A list of territories which permit bearer shares and – what is the U.K.-style equivalent of the bearer share – the share warrant to bearer is shown in paragraph 11. Listed in paragraph 12 are the surprisingly few territories which permit shares of no-par value.

Management and Control; Administrative Offices

After the lists of permitted corporate names and of jurisdictions for Stepping Stones (see p. 71), comes paragraph 15, which lists territories suitable for holding board meetings. Where it is a condition of the tax exemption that the 'management and control' of a company should be elsewhere, the question arises, 'Where?'.

A company which requires to be non-resident for the purposes of the U.K. tax system or of any system having a similar 'management and control' test[15] needs to decide where its board meetings are to be held. They may of course be held in any of the zero-tax jurisdictions, or – provided the company's income arises outside that country – in any of the countries which impose tax on a territorial basis. Other candidates are countries which do not attach importance to the mere holding of board meetings. Thus the board may meet in Monaco, Luxembourg or Switzerland (though in Switzerland there may be an advantage in moving from one Canton to another). In the United States, a foreign company is not taxed unless it carries on business through an office or fixed place of business there, and even then only on income 'effectively connected' with that place of business. Germany seems also a good location, though the German tax authorities are strict, and the company should be ready to show that the day-to-day activities of the company are conducted elsewhere. France is also possible, though it may be prudent not to have regular meetings in the same place. Belgium, the Netherlands and Denmark are possible for occasional and irregular meetings.

The next list is one of countries suitable for administrative offices of companies. It is a perennial problem of international tax planning to obtain tax benefits while at the same time ensuring that the business actually gets done. If the business can be conducted in a zero-tax jurisdiction, or in a territory which confers an exemption from tax on the entity concerned – for instance, the Luxembourg Holding Company, the Gibraltar Exempt Company, or the Hong Kong company whose income arises outside the Colony – no such problem arises. But a company may require to have an office in another country, and again the question arises, 'Where?'

As a place for day-to-day management, one may first consider Monaco, either using a Monegasque management company or an administrative office of the foreign company itself.[16] Andorra can be useful where the company is dealing with property or other matters in Spain or southern France. Jersey and Guernsey permit day-to-day management, provided the company is not doing business there; agreement can be reached with the tax authorities that taxable income of the administrative office will be an agreed percentage of the local outgoings. Similar agreements can be reached in Singapore, the United Kingdom or the Irish Republic. The Greek Government actively encourages foreign companies to establish administrative offices in Greece.[17]

A company may have a mere address in the U.K., Switzerland, Channel Islands, the Irish Republic or Italy. A physical presence may be maintained in limited circumstances in Belgium or in exceptional circumstances in Liechtenstein. In France and Switzerland, a separate service company is to be preferred, as indeed it is generally in other jurisdictions also.

Lastly, there are listed, in paragraphs 18 and 19, places where one can own land, or have a numbered account. In the Bahamas, foreigners require consent to own land, but this can be obtained without much difficulty. In Bermuda, by contrast, consent will only be given in special circumstances. Permission is also required in the British Virgin Islands, and it would be granted for the purchase of vacant land only if the purchaser commits himself to developing the land. There are very severe restrictions in the Channel Islands on the occupation of houses – for there has been for years great pressure from would-be immigrants, but there is no restriction on the *cwnership* of real property.

5. Zero-Tax Jurisdictions

There are two zero-tax territories in the Pacific (Nauru and Vanuatu)[1] and one in the Persian Gulf (Bahrain);[2] but the most numerous, and by far the most important of them, are to be found in the Caribbean, and it is with these territories that this chapter is concerned. They have in common their British connection and their innocence of income tax (Bermuda alone has a tax linked to the income of resident individuals), so that one finds in each of them, very roughly speaking, the same kind of trust and the same kind of company,[3] and – rather more roughly speaking – the same kind of political institutions and general legal framework. It is sometimes said that the Caribbean is an 'American lake', which may give the user of its offshore facilities some reassurance about the future political complexion of the area, but by the same token it is not the place to site a transaction which runs counter to American foreign policies for the time being. So if business is to be done with Cuba or Afghanistan, this may not be the area in which to incorporate the company to do the business. And because there are a lot of black people in these territories, it will be wise to incorporate elsewhere if the business is with South Africa, just as Bahrain is not an ideal place for a transaction with Israel.

This chapter considers not what these territories have in common, but what distinguishes them from one another.[4] What particular merits does each of them have? Given that a transaction could be achieved in any one of them, does one of them have an advantage over the other?

Bermuda

Bermuda (which is not in the Caribbean at all) has two principal features – first, its mid-Atlantic situation and, second, its expertise in the field of insurance. Bermudians are no newcomers to international business: they were selling British gunpowder to the Americans in the War of Independence, were selling everything British to both sides in the American civil war, and established their first exempted company in 1935. Although they have done so very discreetly, they have been hugely successful in selling their facilities to major world-wide enterprises and institutions, and they are reputed to enjoy a *per capita* income next only to that of Kuwait. They have no income tax as such, no capital gains tax, no death duties. In *per capita* terms they have one of the world's smallest bureaucracies, and they have an infrastructure, and professional, banking and financial facilities which are unsurpassed by any other small country or island.

Bermuda's geographical situation and its agreeable climate make it a tempting stop-off between London and New York and there are good air links with North America. If, for example, a transaction calls for periodic meetings between North Americans and Englishmen or Europeans, Bermuda could well be the natural place to base it. Moreover, the golf courses and beaches are world-famous, and though one should not go to Bermuda expecting to find hotels and restaurants like the Peninsula or the Pyramide, the tourist facilities – like everything else in Bermuda, from the plumbing to the telephone and telex system – *work*, and things tend to happen when they should.

The pre-eminence of Bermuda in the field of captive insurance has already been briefly mentioned.[5] Bermuda was very much at the centre of the development of the Captive Insurance Company: this movement emanated from the U.S. multinationals, and Bermuda is the offshore financial centre closest to New York. The phrase 'Captive Insurance Company' is used to mean a company established as part of a group of companies doing business in various parts of the world. A Captive today is not only a vehicle for self-insurance, but also a vehicle for buying insurance or reinsurance wholesale and selling it retail, so that the profit arises in a politically stable country and in a convertible currency. Where the Captive has fiscal as well as economic objectives, the profit may suffer either no tax or tax at a rate lower than would have been suffered on the profit forgone by the operating companies in the group – the companies, that is to say, which buy their insurance from the Captive. The use of the Captive is therefore particularly advantageous where the operating companies are doing business in politically unstable countries, and where, if the currency of a country is not fully convertible, consent can nevertheless be obtained for the payment of insurance premiums to a foreign company. The transactions are fiscally effective where the operating company is able to deduct the premium in computing the trading profits for the purposes of its local tax: insofar as the group as a whole undertakes a measure of self-insurance, the use of a Captive converts, in the accounts of the operating company, a contingency reserve into an outgoing, thereby under many systems converting an item which would not be deductible for tax purposes into one which is. In recent years, Guernsey has made a serious bid for the captive business of European groups, with evident success, and insurance operations have been established in several other jurisdictions.[6] But Bermuda is, undoubtedly, well in the lead.

There are now some fifteen to twenty underwriters residing there, and Bermuda has organisations (owned not only by major international brokers but also by local well-qualified, experienced personnel) well equipped to manage Captives and fully fledged insurance and reinsurance and brokerage companies. It is plainly Government policy to encourage the growth of international business and insurance in Bermuda. Though in recent years there has been some shift of clientele away from the United States and towards European and other developed countries, this growth seems likely to continue. The insurance industry and Government confidently state that the annual net premium income of insurance operations in Bermuda in 1981 probably exceeded three billion U.S. dollars. An estimated one billion is held by choice through local banks.

It is usual, in common law jurisdictions, to find in the statute relating to companies a standard form of memorandum of association of the company, which the incorporators are free, within limits, to adopt either wholly or in part. (The articles contain practically everything which is found in the 'Statuts' or 'Statuten' of civil law jurisdictions, except the objects of the company.) This standard form has the merit of reducing very considerably the physical bulk of corporate documents. The Bermudians have carried this idea one step further, by providing a statutory set of powers and objects for their offshore companies. Any other jurisdiction minded to modernise its company law could do worse than take a leaf out of the Bermudians' book. The offshore company in Bermuda is known as an 'Exempted Company'. It is confusing that this phrase 'Exempted Company' should occur in different territories and with a different meaning under different laws.[7] What an Exempted Company in Bermuda is exempt from is the provisions of the Companies Law which restricts to 40 per cent the proportion of the share capital which may be held by non-Bermudians; this exemption is granted on terms. The most important of the terms – looking at the matter from a Bermudian point of view – is that the Exempted Company pays a flat annual fee to Government (on the other hand an undertaking may be obtained against imposition of tax on profits, etc. until the year 2006). The other very important term is that an Exempted Company may not trade or do business in Bermuda except in furtherance of its business outside Bermuda.

The Exempted Company has proved a successful and popular vehicle for offshore business. Bermuda has developed a reputation for not welcoming shady business – indeed, for frightening such business away – but continues to encourage business of high quality.

At all events, it has become the common wisdom in Bermuda that their tax-haven facilities should not be in any sense actively marketed: if people find out that they can have companies and trusts in Bermuda which pay no local tax, that is all very well and good; but to advertise this facility could overstrain the quality of services through rapid expansion or cause adverse reaction in Washington, Ottawa, London or elsewhere.[8] Whether this is right or wrong is for the Bermudians to decide, but it must be conceded that they have attracted a lot of very good business by appearing not to try, and there seems no reason to suppose that they will not continue to succeed.

Another manifestation of Bermudian exclusiveness is the limitation they have placed on banking operations in their islands. After a good deal of agonising, the number of permitted banks was doubled several years ago – that is to say, it went up from two to four. None of the major international banks is represented in Bermuda, although Barclays is a minority shareholder in a local bank; Bank of Nova Scotia and local shareholders sold their bank to one of the old established banks in 1981. Midland Bank has a less than 10 per cent interest in the other old established bank – the Bank of Bermuda; a similarly restrictive policy prevents the well-known trust companies from having an active presence in Bermuda. It follows that if a transaction calls for the participation of any of the international institutions one is probably not going to be able to site it in Bermuda unless in co-operation with one of the three local banks.

Because of its professional facilities Bermuda should be considered particularly where the geography of the transaction makes it a logical centre or where insurance expertise is required. Apart from the Exempted Companies mentioned above, Bermuda has the facilities usually found in Commonwealth countries for the establishment of trusts, together with excellent management and investment advisers. An Exempted and/or Limited Partnership can also be formed in Bermuda – a feature which will be particularly interesting to those concerned with U.K.-resident taxpayers who are not domiciled in any part of the United Kingdom.

The Bahamas

Moving some way to the south (and those familiar with the area only from maps will be amazed how far away it is), one comes next to the Bahamas. The feature of the offshore business in the Bahamas which is immediately striking is its sheer size, and the number of lawyers, accountants, bankers and trust officers it employs. Downtown Nassau is sprinkled with gleaming new buildings, all buzzing with word processors and computer terminals and air-conditioned lifts full of people carrying files and briefcases: one is plainly in the middle of a truly large industry. The Bahamians claim that whatever kind of tax-haven operation is required, they can provide the facilities. To place the odd 100 million dollar loan? They can handle it. A flag of convenience? They have a Shipping Act. Invoicing operations, trust administration, portfolio management? There are numerous institutions to call on. And if an individual wants to retire to the Bahamas, he will find that there are new provisions for permanent residence for persons of adequate means. The number of companies registered there grows annually, and this despite the introduction of an annual registration fee of the equivalent of U.S. $1,000 (which is high in relation to the annual fees charged elsewhere). New banks are establishing themselves, with a real presence, and not merely with brass plates. And although, in the economy in general, unemployment is unfortunately high, in the financial sector qualified staff are hard to come by.

The factor which is entirely left out of this account of the Bahamas is, of course, the political one. With the sudden and rather unexpected coming to power of a new government rather more than a decade ago, there was – perhaps understandably – concern by the financial community about the future, and this was compounded by a more stringent application of immigration and work-permit rules which had the effect of removing from the financial community a great deal of the accumulated expertise of many years. But after a long shake-down and sorting-out period, the Bahamas has emerged, happily, as a very stable place, attracting a lot of new business and likely to attract more business in the future.

One very interesting result of the eclipse of the Bahamas in the early 1970s was that practitioners in the international tax planning field learnt how to manage without them. A lot of business – trust business especially – went to the Cayman Islands. Some business trickled down to the British Virgin Islands, not very much by Nassau standards, but it seemed quite a lot in Tortola, which had previously had virtually no offshore business. But it seems reasonable to suppose that most of the business which left the Bahamas, and, more importantly, much of the *new* business which did not go to the Bahamas, found a home outside the Caribbean altogether. There were a number of offshore territories eager and waiting to pick up business – Gibraltar, Nauru, Vanuatu and others, and some of what would have been Bahamian business went there. But it may have been the upheaval in the Bahamas which stimulated the movement of offshore business away from the zero-tax jurisdictions towards low-tax and even high-tax jurisdictions, which has been such an important feature of the last decade. Once a practitioner discovers that trust business which could be done in Nassau can be done in the Isle of Man, or Switzerland, or even the United Kingdom, he may feel inclined to take new business to those countries. In the companies field also there was something of a retreat from the Caribbean. This was the decade in which the Gibraltar Exempt Company[9] was launched, the Guernsey and Jersey 'corporation tax' company came into prominence, and new offshore territories vied for a share of the business. What happened in this epoch was that many people, who would previously have prescribed a Nassau company almost automatically, educated themselves about the virtues of the alternatives: practitioners began to know more about other countries, about the virtues of being in the same time zone, about the administrative efficiency of other centres and about the cosmetic advantages of avoiding well-known tax havens.

It seems now that this movement away from the Bahamas, and from the Caribbean generally, has gone as far as it is going to go. Whatever the shortcomings of the Government in Nassau, no customer of the Bahamas offshore facilities has had his assets sequestered or frozen or blocked in any way. One hears grotesque stories of the slow pace of the Nassau bureaucrats, but in practice this does not affect the offshore customer and indeed the people at the Central Bank appear from all accounts efficient, accessible, flexible and amazingly quick.

It may be premature to think of Nassau as a location for an insurance operation or a base for a shipping line. But both the Insurance Act and the Shipping Act are complicated pieces of legislation, and the Government has plainly put much effort into getting them on to the statute book: this effort corroborates the statements which Ministers have made from time to time avowing the Government's intention to maintain the country's tax-haven status. Now it is perhaps timely to remind oneself that there are occasions when Nassau is very much the right place for an international transaction. It is the place to choose, first of all (and this appears to be something of a general rule in international tax planning) when the geography of the transaction indicates it. There are direct flights to Canada, the United Kingdom and the United States, and Central and South America are readily accessible via Miami. If the transaction requires that people from those localities get together from time to time then Nassau is a natural location; provided the visitor chooses very carefully where he is going to stay, it is quite a nice place to go, and if he is someone who would otherwise be spending January in Montreal, it is an extremely nice place to go.

The amenities of Nassau (golf courses, shopping, schooling) and of course the climate make the Bahamas attractive to executives located there. The other main reason for locating in the Bahamas is its very extensive facilities: the leading international accounting firms and the international banks and trust companies are all to be found in Nassau. This may point to a location in Nassau as a matter of convenience, or even as a matter of necessity. If for example one is involved in a transaction with an institution in a major centre like Nassau, it may be a term of the agreement that a company be incorporated for the purpose in the same centre.[10]

Turks and Caicos Islands

At the south-east tip of the Bahamas archipelago, is to be found one of the newest entrants to the tax-haven business – the Turks and Caicos Islands. This is a British colony, with essentially English laws and institutions. It has the same freedom from income tax and other taxes as the territories already mentioned, and no meaningful industry except tourism and fishing: it is rather in the state the Cayman Islands was in a dozen or so years ago. However, the local currency is the U.S. dollar and Government has made a point of welcoming offshore business, and these features in themselves have begun to attract a certain amount of company formation business. For some time, this territory has had a regular air-link with Miami and has offered a comparatively cheap company incorporation service; since there are relatively few companies registered there, one can expect to have less difficulty in getting approval for a desired name for a company than one may experience in the larger centres.

The passing of the 1981 Companies Ordinance has considerably enhanced the attraction of Turks and Caicos as a jurisdiction for company incorporation. Before introducing the new law, the Government took the views of a number of practitioners in the international tax planning field, and the Ordinance embodies several features from the laws of other jurisdictions. The Ordinance has simplified incorporation procedure; it permits bearer shares, redeemable shares and shares of no-par value; it allows the *ultra vires* doctrine to be excluded. A company must keep accounts but these are not available to the public. The Ordinance also introduces the category of Exempted Company. A company may qualify as Exempted if its business is mainly outside the Colony. The name of an Exempted Company need not end in 'Limited'; it may contain other designations (for example, Inc., AG, BV, NV), but need not. An Exempted Company may transfer its domicil into and out of the Islands; it need not file annual returns, nor is it required to maintain a register of or make public the names of its directors or shareholders. It must, however, maintain a registered office in the Islands and appoint a local agent, to be responsible for filing an annual Declaration of Compliance and to accept on behalf of the company service of any proceedings. Exempted Companies have a guaranteed freedom from tax for twenty years, and breaches of confidentiality and unauthorised disclosure of information concerning the affairs of Exempted Companies are severely punishable by law.

Anguilla

Anguilla sprang into brief prominence a decade ago, by staging the world's first and only anti-decolonisation rebellion. It is once again a British colony. Its Income Tax Ordinance was suspended in 1977,[11] and it has since then attracted a small amount of company incorporation business. In this field, its competitor is Turks and Caicos: while one cannot yet incorporate in Anguilla with the same speed and efficiency which is available in Turks and Caicos, the Colony does have the advantage of being accessible to the other territories which feature in the international tax planner's world – St Martin (the Dutch part of which is comprised in the Netherlands Antilles) being just across the water, and the British and United States Virgin Islands being only minutes' flying-time away.

Cayman Islands

Fifteen years ago the Cayman Islands was the sort of place where one could take a siesta in the middle of the main street with no risk of being run over. Today, Cayman is a kind of miniature Bahamas. It has branches of many of the same British and North American banks which have offices in the Bahamas – and their associated trust corporations also; and it has the same absence of taxes, the same English common law. But everything about Cayman is smaller – the land area, the population, the hotels, the size of Georgetown, its principal city. The great advantage of this smallness lies in the ease with which it is possible to do business there. Everybody is extremely accessible – lawyers, bankers, accountants and, most remarkably perhaps, Government. If a transaction requires a meeting with the Registrar of Trusts or the Registrar of Shipping or the Financial Secretary or even the Governor, this can be arranged, with the minimum of fuss and an incredible absence of red tape. Although

Government maintains a discreet and dignified posture, the fact is that everyone from His Excellency downwards feels it part of his job to promote the Colony as a tax haven. They began, in 1961, with a Companies Law – a flexible, usable law – perhaps a little light on winding-up provisions (which is to be remedied) but excellent for its purpose. The Companies Law was followed in 1967 by the Trusts Law. By the end of the 1960s they had legislation to regulate banks and trust companies on the same pattern as the Bahamian Law – and there is now understood to be some measure of co-operation between the two Registrars. This involvement on the part of Government has been a continuous feature of the development of the Colony as a tax haven and financial centre. They were blessed with a particularly able Caymanian Financial Secretary, Vassal Johnson, who held office throughout this period, and who may well be regarded as the true architect of their success in this field.

Like Bermuda, the Cayman Islands have in their law the expression 'Exempted Company'. The features which a Caymanian company has in common with its Bermudian namesake is a restriction on trading locally, an obligation to pay a special fee to Government each year and the right to an undertaking from Government that if income taxes are imposed in the future, the company will be exempt from them – in Bermuda until 2006 and in Cayman usually for twenty years from the date of incorporation. But there the resemblance to Bermuda ends, for the Cayman company is emancipated from statutory requirements to a degree unparalleled in any common law jurisdiction. Its name need not end with 'Limited', it has greater freedom than has the ordinary Caymanian company to change its objects and the location of its registered office; it may reduce its capital without the consent of the Court; the number of members can be reduced to one (though this may be inconvenient, for the company cannot hold a meeting unless it has at least two members); no disclosure of shareholders is required; it may issue bearer and no-par value shares.

Four types of 'trust' may be created under Cayman Islands' law:

1. An ordinary trust.
2. An exempted trust.
3. A section 77 exempted trust.
4. A section 79 exempted trust.

These have the following features.

An ordinary trust may be created in any form permissible under English law.

A trust may be registered as an exempted trust under Part V of the Trusts Law (Appendix 3). This differs from an ordinary trust in three respects:

(i) The original trust instrument is lodged in a file kept by the Registrar of Trusts; the file is not open to public inspection, nor to inspection by anyone other than the trustees and persons expressly authorised by the trust instrument.

(ii) Registration and annual fees are payable to the Registrar of Trusts.

(iii) The Governor of the Cayman Islands may give an undertaking, exempting for a period, not exceeding fifty years, the trust property and income from any taxes imposed in the future in the Cayman Islands. As a matter of practice the Governor does give such an undertaking.

A 'section 77' exempted trust is one approved under section 77 of the Trusts Law 1967 in advance of being created. This differs from other exempted trusts in that the exemption from tax is given in advance. A further advantage of a section 77 trust is that it may have a perpetuity period[12] of a specified number of years not exceeding one hundred.

A 'section 79' exempted trust must contain at least some discretionary trust or power to appoint or apply capital or income to or for the benefit of the beneficiaries. It has the same features as a section 77 exempted trust, with two important differences:

(i) It is not capable of being varied by the Court under Part IV of the Trusts Law 1967.

(ii) No beneficiary has any right to enforce the trust, whether he has under the terms of the trust instrument a vested or contingent or other interest, or merely an expectancy as the object of a power or discretion. The trustees may be sued for breach of trust only by their successors as trustees or by the Registrar of Trusts. No beneficiary is entitled to any information, or to inspect or to copy documents, relating to the trust.

The practical importance of a section 79 trust is that it enables a settlor to confer benefits on children or on adult beneficiaries of unsound mind or weak personality or on individuals he thinks might turn out to be greedy or grasping, without giving them any right in law to apply to the Court or otherwise make nuisances of themselves in the event that the Trustees decide not to exercise their discretion in their favour.

Evidently, a good deal of new business in Cayman has come from major corporations, including a certain amount of Captive and other insurance business, and there are now firms there which specialise in the management of insurance operations. But the true strength of Cayman lies in its ability to do private client business – setting up a trust to administer a portfolio or a company to handle a transaction. It is not altogether easy to reach – but then, neither is Liechtenstein. The hotels, if a little primitive, are pleasant. People are friendly. And indeed there is a pervasive air of lack of formality which is rivalled in this area only by the British Virgin Islands (see p. 46).

6. Tax Treaties

A resident of country A, with a source of income in country B, may be liable to tax in both countries: in A because of his residence, and in B because of the source. The purpose of the by now very numerous tax treaties is to prevent this double taxation. The general principle adopted is that the source tax should give way to the residence tax. A tax treaty, if it applies to a taxpayer at all, is always beneficial to him: the treaties do not impose any tax, but give relief by way of credit or exemption. The most advantageous circumstances to the taxpayer are those where he is exempt from the source tax by the treaty, while not being liable to any, or to any significant, residence tax.

This chapter begins with some examples of such advantageous combinations, and then considers examples with a common characteristic, under the heading 'The Stepping Stone'. As regards the United Kingdom, at least, the treaty may confer upon a resident an exemption from his residence tax, although this result does not appear to have been intended.[1]

Treaties and Low-Tax Entities

It is a feature of a number of treaties to which Switzerland is a party that a partnership organised under Swiss law is to be treated as a 'resident of Switzerland' for the purposes of the treaty, and will therefore be entitled to the usual exemption from any tax on business profits (in the absence of a permanent establishment) which would, but for the treaty, be levied by the treaty partner.[2] But a Swiss partnership in the form of a *société-simple* is not a tax-paying entity and non-resident partners in a Swiss partnership are not liable to tax, unless the partnership is treated under the (rather liberal) Swiss rules as having a place of business in Switzerland.

U.S. partnerships have a similar fiscal transparency, but nevertheless benefit as residents of the United States under some of the older American treaties. As has already been mentioned, a U.K.-resident trustee, who is, as 'a resident of the United Kingdom', exempt from capital gains tax otherwise leviable by the treaty partner, may nevertheless be treated for domestic purposes as non-resident.[3]

A Dutch company which functions as a holding company[4] is not, like its Luxembourg equivalent, excluded from the benefit of tax treaties. In most Dutch tax treaties (but not in the treaty with Germany) dividend-withholding taxes are reduced to 5 per cent or less where a 25 per cent participation in the foreign company is held. Since the recent revision of the Anglo-Dutch Treaty, it has become difficult for residents of third countries (other than those with which the United Kingdom has a treaty dealing with Advance Corporation Tax) to use a Netherlands holding company to reclaim tax on U.K. dividends; but where it can be done, it is a singularly advantageous structure, for, since advance corporation tax is creditable against the mainstream corporation tax on the U.K. company's underlying activities, the effect of the structure can be to reduce the tax payable in the United Kingdom from 52 to 43 per cent (or, where the Netherlands company and its associates have less than 10 per cent of the voting power in the U.K. company, to 39 per cent).[5]

In the Netherlands Antilles, as already mentioned,[6] a company must deny itself the benefit of the special low-tax regime if it is to enjoy all the benefits of the treaties with the United Kingdom and the United States, but low-tax companies may still be (and not uncommonly are) used as vehicles for property development in the United Kingdom and real estate investment in the United States.[7]

Where the two or more low-tax or zero-tax entities are co-operating in a business venture, they may consider the formation of a Danish co-operative. The co-operative in Denmark, while obtaining benefits under the numerous treaties to which Denmark is a party, suffers tax in Denmark, as already mentioned,[8] only on a notional basis.

The Offshore Company in Cyprus[9] also has the feature of paying a low rate of local tax, while enjoying the benefits of most of Cyprus's tax treaties, that is, those with Czechoslovakia,

Denmark, East and West Germany, Greece, Hungary, Ireland, Norway, Romania and Sweden; it also enjoys some benefits of the treaty with France and the United Kingdom. The list of treaty partners compares favourably with those of other low-tax jurisdictions, and further treaties await signature and ratification.

With the termination by the United States of the extensions of the old U.K. treaty to colonial territories, the International Business Company in Barbados (paying local tax at a rate which does not exceed $2\frac{1}{2}$ per cent[10] but nevertheless a 'resident' for treaty purposes) has lost a good deal of its interest. Nevertheless, a Barbados IBC may still be a useful vehicle for Canadian residents,[11] or for doing business with any of the Scandinavian countries (with whom the extensions of U.K. treaties still stand).

There is the occasional anomaly to be found in the different treatment accorded to an item of income by the domestic law of the recipient on the one hand and by the law of the jurisdiction granting the relief or exemption under the treaty, on the other. In the United States, for example, interest paid by a partnership to a partner is not treated as a distribution of a share of profits. A German resident partner therefore receives interest exempt under the U.S. treaty, which interest is deductible in computing the profits of the partnership for U.S. tax purposes; the German tax treatment of such interest payments has not been tested in the Courts, but it appears that they should be treated as a partnership distribution, and be free of German tax accordingly (but nevertheless be taken into account in determining the rate of tax on his taxable income).

The profits of a foreign branch of a Swiss company can be free of Swiss tax, but if the branch is in the United States, it is liable to U.S. tax only on its income from U.S. sources and not on 'effectively connected' income. This suggests the possibility of a Swiss company with an office in New York doing business with customers outside the United States.[12] (An office of a Netherlands Antilles enterprise may be considered as an alternative.)

The Stepping Stone

There is a class of transaction which takes advantage of the interaction between domestic law and treaty benefits in a different way; this involves the use of what has become known as the

'Stepping Stone'. This transaction is of importance primarily where interest or royalties have their source in high-tax countries.

A Stepping Stone does not enjoy any kind of low-tax regime. Its essential qualities are two: first, it must be situated in a jurisdiction which imposes no withholding tax on its outward payments, and secondly its inward payments must be received free of withholding or other tax in their place of origin, by virtue of the provisions of the relevant tax treaty. The payment of interest or royalties from a high-tax country (Country H) to a low-tax country (Country L) may involve withholding tax in Country H. The Stepping Stone structure involves a payment from Country H to the Stepping Stone, which is made without deduction of tax by virtue of the tax treaty between Country H and the Stepping Stone country, and an onward payment from the Stepping Stone country to Country L, which is made gross by virtue of the absence of any withholding requirement or other liability to tax in the Stepping Stone country. The Netherlands may be used for interest and royalties,[13] Luxembourg for interest on short-term borrowing but not royalties,[14] the United Kingdom for interest and some royalties (but not patent royalties or copyright royalties),[15] and Denmark for royalties but not (for reasons not of tax but of exchange control) for interest.[16] What the Stepping Stone countries have in common is that they are all high-tax jurisdictions. It is therefore of great importance, from the point of view of the Stepping Stone company itself, that it can deduct against the inward payments the whole of the outward payments. Difficulties in this area seem to be most easily overcome where the Stepping Stone is wholly independent of both the original payer and the ultimate payee, because so long as its relationship with these other two parties is a purely commercial one it has no reason to make outgoing payments except those which can be justified on purely commercial grounds. On the other hand, it is never wise to choose a Stepping Stone simply on the ground that it charges the lowest turn or spread: an essential requirement of a viable Stepping Stone is that it not only be credible and honest but also solvent, and a Stepping Stone which trims its margins too fine can all too easily find in practice that its operating expenses exceed its gross profit. But there is also a tax consideration here: in order to obtain the benefit of the relevant treaty, the Stepping Stone company may well need the help and co-operation of its own tax authorities, and those authorities are – to put it no higher – more likely to be helpful if they can see that they themselves are getting a reasonable amount of tax out of the transaction. In the Netherlands, it is possible to obtain a formal ruling, and in Denmark an informal one.

There are certain companies which have made something of a speciality in the business of acting as a Stepping Stone. A person intending to enter into a transaction of this kind may, of course, always incorporate a company of his own for the purpose. Although, as has already been mentioned, an independent Stepping Stone has the advantage that its outgoings cannot be challenged on the grounds of non-commerciality, the choice between the two will be governed largely by commercial considerations. An 'in-house' Stepping Stone will be indicated in cases where the marketing of the product requires the Stepping Stone company to have a distinctive name, or to acquire premises and staff for the unique purpose of handling the transaction concerned. At the same time, it is likely to be more expensive to administer a separate company for a particular transaction than to make use of the services of an independent company which has been handling transactions of this kind for some years. Where the expertise of an established organisation is particularly valuable is in the handling of the money movements: if these are not policed with great promptness and effectiveness, it is all too easy for money to be 'lost' in the banking system for weeks at a time, the lost interest on which can add very considerably to the cost of the transaction.

The principle of the Stepping Stone can be applied also in self-insurance. Where an individual, or family or group of individuals or indeed companies have assets in the ownership of an offshore company or trust, but commercial or professional activities in one or more high-tax territories, it may be desirable to utilise the offshore assets as the backing for at any rate some part of the insurance – product liability, professional negligence or other – required by the business or profession. Looked at from the point of view of the offshore structure, such a transaction has an effect similar to that of an individual's membership of a syndicate at Lloyds: the assets are placed doubly at risk – once in the investment, and a second time as backing for the insurance – and yield a correspondingly large income. As with members at Lloyds, a significant part of the increased yield is attributable to the insurer's ability to invest for his own benefit the premiums which he collects, and to retain these investments until the day arrives when they are required to meet a claim. The transaction looked at as a whole has something of the characteristics of Captive insurance: the premiums may effectively cross an exchange control frontier, and they may be deductible in computing the profits of the business or profession in the high-tax territory, while not being subject to tax in the territory in which they are received. A Stepping Stone is indicated in cases where the high-tax territory concerned imposes a withholding or other tax on outgoing premiums, but a lower rate of tax is payable under a treaty. Thus it is advantageous to utilise a United Kingdom insurance Stepping Stone where premiums emanate from the United States. It may still be advantageous to use a Stepping Stone, even in cases where withholding tax on premiums is levied, so long as the Stepping Stone company obtains a tax credit for the tax withheld, which would be of no value to the reinsurer in the zero-tax jurisdiction.

Here again, anyone contemplating such a transaction has the alternative of forming his own Stepping Stone or utilising the services of an existing organisation. Whereas the directors of a Stepping Stone company which is, say, granting licences to make recordings of popular music, do not need to know very much about either recording or popular music, the directors of a company handling such an insurance transaction do need to have some knowledge of insurance, if only in order to ensure that the Stepping Stone company reinsures at Lloyds or elsewhere the risks which cannot be borne by the offshore structure. It seems in practice, therefore, that such transactions are for the most part undertaken by independent Stepping Stone companies, which have acquired the necessary experience in this field.

The U.S. Treasury has become increasingly sensitive to what it regards as abuse of tax treaties, that is their use to benefit, indirectly, residents of third-party countries – the so-called 'treaty shopping'. It seems likely that future treaties with the U.S. will contain anti-treaty-shopping articles of some kind or another. One may expect the United States, consistently with such a policy towards new treaty partners, to make considerable efforts to eliminate the treaty shopping possibilities present in its existing treaties – notably in that with the Netherlands Antilles. But the attempt to pursue such a policy appears to be arousing considerable opposition, not only from the treaty partner countries themselves, but from the large American corporations, a substantial part of whose loan capital has been financed through Antilles subsidiaries. As a practical matter, the only conclusion which seems capable of being drawn at the time of writing is that this is an area in which the practitioner ought to be prepared for change: where U.S.-source income is concerned, any transaction whose effectiveness depends upon treaty shopping should be a short-term transaction or, at least, one capable of termination. This is a subject which is rife with rumour and speculation, but it may be reasonable to assume that if the U.S. Treasury pursues a course of renegotiating treaties, the first on the list will be those with treaty partners which have lent themselves to this device on a large scale (notably the Netherlands and the Netherlands Antilles),[17] and on that basis the practitioner would do well to seek out countries where this form of transaction is, if not unknown, at least unusual.

7. Offshore Trusts

Readers whose background and training is in the civil law may be pardoned if they find the English concept of the *trust* hard to grasp; a few words about its nature may therefore be helpful here.

A trust is said to exist where a person who is the owner of an asset ('the trustee') holds it not for his own benefit but for the benefit of one or other persons ('the beneficiaries'). So far as the outside world is concerned, the trustee is the true owner of the asset: he can, for example, sell it, and pass a good title to the purchaser. But he is accountable to his beneficiaries for his actions: if he held the asset on trust before the sale, he afterwards holds the proceeds of sale on trust. In this context, it is useful to think of a trust as a continuing entity, like a company, and of its assets ('the trust fund') being in the continuing ownership of such a body, despite changes in their identity, and indeed despite changes in the identity of the trustees themselves. But a trust is not in law a separate body; it is a set of obligations undertaken by the trustee with respect to the trust fund. The trustee undertakes these obligations in the first place by contract with the person who provided the assets ('the settlor'). It is a distinguishing feature of a trust, however, that performance of these obligations can be enforced by persons who are not parties to the contract, namely, the beneficiaries.

The concept of the trust has become part of the law of the very numerous tax havens which have an historical connection with the United Kingdom. It is customary in those territories for the obligations of the trustee to be undertaken, not by individuals, but by corporations which make a business of doing so, and the trust has proved to be a most flexible and adaptable vehicle for placing the ownership of assets in the hands of corporations in the tax havens, subject to the obligation – which the Courts will be ready to enforce – to hold such assets for the benefit of beneficiaries residing elsewhere. Such a trust is sometimes called an 'Offshore Trust'.

The classic function of the Offshore Trust is to make financial provision for members of a kinship group in a way calculated to survive a variety of political events – war, currency erosion, a *coup d'état*, or political or racial persecution. But even where no such event is foreseen, the head of a family may well take the view that some part at least of the assets upon which the family collectively depends should be held outside and independently of the jurisdiction in which he lives – particularly if the assets are situated outside the jurisdiction, or if some members of the family reside elsewhere.

The usual form of Offshore Trust is an accumulation and discretionary settlement, established in a jurisdiction other than that in which the settlor lives. The 'host country' will either have a zero-tax regime, or impose no tax on trust capital, income or capital gains. Characteristically, the trust instrument will empower the trustees, or impose on them the duty, to accumulate the trust income during the whole of the perpetuity period;[1] the trustees will have power, at their discretion, to distribute capital or income or both to beneficiaries while the trust is in existence, and will be required to distribute – at their discretion – the capital among the beneficiaries, or some of them, upon the termination of the trust. The trustees will commonly be given wide powers of investment, including powers to form companies, and the trust instrument will contain provisions for apportionment between income and capital, for the holding of trust investments in nominees' names, for dealing with land and buildings, for acquiring and holding chattels, for the trustees to borrow, for remuneration of the trustees, etc., in a fashion not very dissimilar from trusts established in high-tax jurisdictions.[2] There are, however, three features of an Offshore Trust not commonly encountered in domestic trusts – a provision for changing the place in which the trust is administered, a provision establishing the office of Protector and a power to the trustees to add beneficiaries.

There is now a wide choice of host countries, but in assessing the relative political merits of these by now somewhat competitive territories, it is probably not possible, in the present state of the world, to attempt a long-term view, and it is in recognition of this that the trust instrument will generally contain a mechanism whereby a person not subject to the jurisdiction of the host country has power to change the trustees or otherwise remove the trust from that jurisdiction.[3] Some draftsmen include a provision enabling the person outside the host country to change the law governing the trust. It is not altogether easy to see what the effect of such a purported change may be,[4] but, as a practical matter, the important effect to be achieved is that the trust assets should be capable of being dealt with by the successor trustees in the manner which the trust instrument originally envisaged, and that the person actually having control of the title deeds or share certificates or bullion, or whatever the trust assets consist of, can be relied upon to recognise the title of the new trustees quickly and without argument. On the other hand, while political upheaval is not altogether impossible in any country of the world today, the holder of such a power ought to be able to anticipate any such events and ought to be able to exercise his power well before any serious situation arises.

The function of the Protector is to act as a kind of liaison officer between the trustees and the beneficiaries. It is unusual nowadays, in any of the offshore jurisdictions where trusts are established, to find individuals acting as trustees; generally a trust corporation is appointed the sole trustee, and the officers of that corporation may change from time to time. Here the choice is between the large organisations, generally owned by one or more banks of international standing, and the smaller trust company, which will be owned by one or a few individuals. There are advantages and disadvantages to both kinds of corporate trustee, but neither can be expected to maintain any very close familiarity with the needs and desires of the individuals who are to benefit under the trust. Typically, the Protector is a relative or close friend of the family whose members constitute the beneficiaries, and the officer of the trust corporation having the responsibility of administration of the trust will confer with him before acceding to any request from the beneficiaries concerning any major change in the conduct of the affairs of the trust or any distribution to the beneficiaries. He will often be the person empowered to change the *situs* of the trust and to remove and appoint trustees, and he should be capable of exercising these powers wisely, when and if the needs of the beneficiaries require.

It is possible for the settlor to confer upon the trustees power to add beneficiaries to the trust. Quite how wide such powers may be is not altogether easy to state. Partly for that reason, it is submitted that this is a feature best avoided, unless the criteria upon which the new beneficiaries are to be chosen is clearly stated in the trust instrument. But it may be desirable to avoid such a feature for another reason also: where the true reason for the insertion of such a power is to enable a trust which is really for X, Y and Z to look as if it were for the benefit of A, B and C, one is in the world of sham and possible fraud, and indeed it would be difficult to have any confidence in the integrity of any trustee who was willing to be party to such deception.[5]

The Settlor

One aspect of the Offshore Trust which can be of crucial importance is the identity of the settlor.[6] If the beneficiaries are Canadian residents, it is advantageous for the settlor not to be a resident of Canada; if the beneficiaries are U.K. residents, the ideal settlor will be neither ordinarily resident nor domiciled in the United Kingdom; and if the beneficiaries are U.S. citizens or residents, the ideal settlor is a person neither a citizen of nor resident in the United States.[7] In this context, the 'settlor' is not simply the person who appears as such on the face of the instrument, and provides at most a nominal starting fund for the trust: he is the person who provides the whole of the trust assets. Where a beneficiary is resident in Canada or the United Kingdom, or a citizen of or resident in the United States, the extent to which he can make available to the trustees, or to companies controlled by the trustees, his knowledge and expertise, without any adverse fiscal consequence, can be a delicate question, and needs to be answered on the facts of each particular case. But where and to the extent that it can be done, the provision of such knowledge and expertise may have the consequence of increasing substantially the value of the fund owned (directly or indirectly) by the trustees of the settlement.

This ideal settlor, who is not resident in, or not domiciled in or not a national of, the country where the beneficiaries are living, is sometimes referred to as 'Uncle George'. Typically, Uncle George is both well heeled and well disposed; he is free of currency control; and no adverse fiscal consequences flow to him by reason of the establishment of the trust. In this context, it is useful to remember that many interests in settlements are capable of being bought and sold, so that beneficiaries who do not have an Uncle George of their own may acquire interests in an existing settlement, and indeed where the size of trust fund required is such as to be well beyond the munificence of any prospective Uncle George, the acquisition by purchase may be their only way of obtaining an interest in an 'Uncle George' settlement.

Offshore Trusts are commonly established in connection with some, or some intended, business activities. There are several possible relationships between the Offshore Trust and the business activities. The trustee may do no more than receive royalties or licence fees, perhaps via a Stepping Stone.[8] Or, as already mentioned, the trustee may itself carry on a trade or may be a partner or a limited partner in a Swiss or other partnership which carries on a trade.[9] But the typical structure is a combination between a trust and a company – the trust being established in a zero-tax jurisdiction, and having as its principal function the holding of shares in one or more operating companies – these being sited in the same or another zero-tax jurisdiction or under a low-tax regime with treaty benefits or elsewhere as the circumstances of the case demand.

Situs

The jurisdictions commonly used for the siting of Offshore Trusts are listed in paragraph 10 of Appendix 1. By far the largest share of the world's Offshore Trust business is conducted in, or at least by companies incorporated in, parts of the British Commonwealth. This is partly an accident of history, most colonies having no income tax until after the Second World War, and the British taking the common law and equity with them to settled colonies, and enacting English-style laws in conquered ones. But it also appears to have been encouraged by the Foreign and Commonwealth Office as a way of generating employment and government revenue in colonial and dependent territories. In the event, the world of the Offshore Trust is not merely a world of the English language but essentially a world of English law. Minor variations between one overseas territory and another exist,[10] but their only substantial difference from England in this regard is that (apart from Hong Kong) they permit accumulation throughout the perpetuity period. Some of the overseas territories have never adopted the income tax. These are the zero-tax jurisdictions of the Caribbean, discussed in Chapter 5. Those which introduced income tax did so by enacting what were essentially simplified versions of the tax system in force in the United Kingdom. In the United Kingdom, as has already been mentioned (p. 28), a trust is treated as a taxpaying entity, and U.K.-resident trustees have always been liable to income tax (at a flat rate) on trust income, regardless of the source of that income, and regardless of the residence of the beneficiaries. The exception to this rule is the treatment of the 'Interest in Possession trust' – that is, one where there is a life tenant or other beneficiary entitled to the income as it arises. In such a case, if the trust income arises outside the United Kingdom, it may be paid direct to a non-resident life tenant without incurring any charge to U.K. tax. The practice in the taxpaying territories on this list – the British Virgin Islands, Cyprus, Gibraltar, the Isle of Man and Jersey[11] – is to treat the exemption as the rule, and to regard all trusts as fiscally transparent, so long as they have non-resident beneficiaries and their income arises outside the territory. The practice is by now so well established in these territories, and such a large amount of trust business depends upon it, that it is most unlikely to be changed (unless it be by legislation to enshrine the practice in the law). Where a U.K. resident trustee carries on an active business for the benefit of the trust fund the trading income is regarded as having its source in the United Kingdom;[12] in these territories, however, it seems that so long as all the customers are outside the jurisdiction, and the trade is not in any local product, the tax authorities can in practice be persuaded to regard the profits as arising abroad for these purposes. Trust income is not taxed in the other countries on this list, at least so long as it arises outside the country in question, though the reasons for this immunity vary from country to country.

Monaco does not impose income tax as such. It does have a 35 per cent business profits tax, on the profits of business (other than local business) carried on there. This tax was brought in to prevent the obvious exploitation of Monaco's tax-free situation by the formation of local companies to do business with other countries – France in particular. But there is no local tax on the income of trusts established there. That the law of Monaco recognises trusts is surprisingly little known, and for this reason their Law 214 of 1936 is reproduced in Appendix 4. One can see that the draftsman was not altogether familiar with Anglo-Saxon legal concepts: he rather untidily assumed that an individual's citizenship determines the nature of the settlement he may make, whereas the English rule is that this is governed by his domicil. But this seems to be easily overcome in practice. It will be observed that there are provisions imposing a tax on the trust fund; this, however, is effectively a tax only on the initial trust fund, and if there are later additions to the trust fund, the law does not impose any tax on those.

Liechtenstein law recognises a somewhat confusing variety of entities, but for practical purposes the choice lies between:

(*a*) The 'Foundation' (*Stiftung*), especially in the form of a 'Family Foundation', which is quite similar to a family trust but using civil law principles.

(*b*) The 'Establishment' (*Anstalt*), a very flexible form of company found only in Liechtenstein law.

(*c*) The Company limited by Shares (*Aktiengesellschaft*), a form of company well known in other countries; the Liechtenstein form is quite different in details.

(*d*) The Trust (*Treuhänderschaft*), nearly identical with the Anglo-Saxon concept of the trust.

(*e*) The Business Trust (*Treuunternehmen*), an American form of trust which is used for commercial activities; in Liechtenstein administration of assets and similar is also permitted.

As in Monaco, a trust in Liechtenstein may import the provisions of English or other foreign law (no limitation being placed in Liechtenstein on the law which may be chosen).

Liechtenstein companies require at least one director who is resident internally and fulfils certain professional requirements. The same applies to trusts which are subject to Liechtenstein law.

The trustees must either enter on the Commercial Register (which is open to inspection by the public) the name, date and duration of the trust, together with their names and addresses or deposit a part of the trust instrument (which need not contain any secret details) with the Court – the instrument in those circumstances not being available to public inspection. There is an annual fee of 1000 Swiss francs (which is in theory a minimum fee though in practice rarely exceeded).

Switzerland does not feature in this list, because its laws do not include the concept of trusts as such. It is understood, however, that the Swiss Court will require a trustee to carry out fiduciary duties which he has undertaken, and a good deal of trust administration is now carried on in Switzerland. For tax purposes, Switzerland treats a trust as transparent, and income from outside Switzerland which enures for the benefit of non-residents is not subject to any municipal, Cantonal or Federal tax.

General Considerations

It will be evident from this short review of jurisdictions appropriate to the establishment of Offshore Trusts that the facilities they offer are not fundamentally different. In deciding between them, the questions to be asked are essentially those of a practical nature. Does the Protector live in the same time zone as the trustee? Do they speak the same language? Are there individuals with whom he can establish the necessary rapport? Is the trust likely to be affected by political changes? Similar questions require to be considered when a company is to be formed – and perhaps with even greater care, for it is more difficult to relocate a company than to relocate a trust.[13] But here one needs to emancipate oneself from the simple notion that companies and trusts are always run in the places under whose laws they are created. Just as one might have a trust established under the law of the Cayman Islands but administered by a trustee resident in Switzerland, so one may have a company incorporated in the Turks and Caicos Islands but administered in Monte Carlo.

The Offshore Company

Where the trust assets are to be invested in a business, it is usual for the trustees to incorporate a company for the purpose, and such a company will generally be incorporated or resident in an appropriate low-tax or zero-tax jurisdiction. Such 'offshore' company may also be utilised to hold investments in real property or other assets.

Every adviser will nowadays be aware of a pervasive, and increasing, public disapproval of the use of the tax havens. True, it still seems to be respectable to establish a unit trust or mutual fund in a tax haven, and the public will take in its stride a Bermudian company engaged in insurance or reinsurance business, or a bond offering from the Netherlands Antilles, or a Hong Kong company dealing in goods made in China, or a Bahamian company selling rum. But companies incorporated in tax havens, whose business has no very apparent connection with the country in which they are incorporated, are mostly to be found nowadays in activities not involving the public. Such companies may hold and manage portfolios, or be the collecting vehicle for a 'back-to-back' borrowing transaction or a 'Stepping Stone' transaction. Companies dealing with the public are mostly incorporated in the jurisdictions where their customers reside, and so far as the international tax planning aspect of the matter goes, their proprietors are likely to think in terms of royalties, interest, transfer pricing and other ways of limiting their exposure to tax in that jurisdiction.

Too many structures of this kind, which look so convincing on paper – with well-drafted trust instruments and well-sited operating companies – fail for lack of what can only be called 'reality'. This is one of those qualities which are easier to recognise than to define. If there are to be meetings, let there be real meetings, with real decisions taken by informed people, and not three seasick lawyers signing a draft minute on the quayside in Sark. If there is to be an office, let it have a number in the phone book, and a person behind the door when one opens it, who is actually doing something and knows what he is doing. Let the operation, whatever its fiscal purpose, have a business purpose. And above all, while no one would suggest that a copy of every document and a transcript of every phone call be sent to the tax authorities of all relevant taxing jurisdictions, let the transaction be conducted so that the transaction is calculated to achieve its fiscal objectives if that were done. All these things, of course, cost money, and this may be one of the reasons why, on the whole, the large and multi-national corporations appear to be more adept at achieving their fiscal objectives than are many smaller enterprises. But perhaps there is another factor here, and that is that larger organisations tend to recognise more readily that there is an amount of tax to be paid and an amount of tax to be saved. International tax planning is not in principle about paying no tax anywhere. Sometimes this happens, but it is very much the exception. In most cases, there will be a necessary exposure to significant amounts of tax: if some part of the transaction can be conducted in a low-tax or zero-tax jurisdiction, it may be expected that the profits of that part of the transaction may be lightly taxed or not taxed at all. That is the ambition which the kind of structure described in this chapter aims to achieve, and even that modest ambition requires that the offshore components do genuinely emanate from the jurisdictions from which they purport to come.

Accumulation

The typical result of an operation of an offshore structure is that the individual finds himself or his family with what may be seen (leaving technicalities aside) as two jars of money – the old money in a tax-prone situation, and the new money in a tax-exempt situation. One may be surprised how many people who are able to accumulate offshore commissions or trading profits or other kinds of new money agonise about how to get that money back into their own hands without paying tax on it, and do not consider the possibility of reducing their domestic fortune by spending it and simply allowing the offshore money to accumulate. In most countries (even in the United Kingdom, with its decidedly stringent capital transfer tax) this technique of filling a new jar while emptying an old one can be used as a way of passing assets to the next generation, without suffering the taxes normally payable on death. There may be an income tax charge at the time when the ultimate recipient gets the money: that will depend on his residence (or in the case of the U.S. on his citizenship) at the time, and it may be worth his while to change that, for whatever period may be requisite.[14]

APPENDIX I

Jurisdictions and Entities

1. *Zero-Tax Jurisdictions for Companies*

Anguilla
Bahamas
Bahrain
Bermuda
Cayman
Nauru
Turks and Caicos
Vanuatu

2. *Taxing Jurisdictions with Exemptions*

Antigua
Barbados
Cook Islands
Cyprus
Denmark
Djibouti
Gibraltar
Grenada
Isle of Man
Israel
St Vincent
Seychelles
Switzerland

3. *Holding Companies*

Liechtenstein
Luxembourg
Nauru
Netherlands
Netherlands Antilles
Switzerland

4. *Non-resident Companies*

Antigua
Barbados
British Virgin Islands
Gibraltar
Grenada
Guernsey
Isle of Man
Israel
Jersey
Singapore
St Vincent
Swaziland
United Kingdom

5. *Territorial Basis*

Brunei
Costa Rica
Hong Kong
Liberia
Liechtenstein
Malaysia
Netherlands
Panama
Seychelles
Singapore
South Africa
U.S. Virgin Islands

6. *Low Tax with Treaty Relief*

Barbados
British Virgin Islands
Cyprus

Grenada
Netherlands
Netherlands Antilles
Republic of Ireland
St Vincent
Switzerland

7. *Unlimited Companies*

British Virgin Islands
Cook Islands
Costa Rica
Hong Kong
Isle of Man
New Hebrides
Switzerland
Turks and Caicos

8. *Captive Companies*

BANKS
Anguilla
Bahamas
Bahrain
British Virgin Islands
Cayman
Cook Islands
Nauru
New Hebrides
Seychelles
Turks and Caicos

TRUST COMPANIES

With Licence
Anguilla
Bahamas
Cook Islands
Cayman
Monaco
Nauru

Without Licence
Australia
British Virgin Islands
Costa Rica
Cyprus
Gibraltar
Guernsey
Hong Kong
Isle of Man
Jersey
Liechtenstein
Panama
Switzerland
Turks and Caicos
United Kingdom

INSURANCE
Anguilla
Bahamas
Barbados
Bermuda
Cayman
Cook Islands
Cyprus
Gibraltar
Guernsey
Hong Kong
Isle of Man
New Hebrides
Panama

9. *Partnerships*

OPEN
Bahamas
Bermuda
Cayman
Cyprus
Hong Kong
Isle of Man
Liechtenstein
New Hebrides
Panama
Switzerland
Turks and Caicos
United States

LIMITED
Bahamas
Bermuda
Cayman
Costa Rica

Cyprus
Gibraltar
Hong Kong
Isle of Man
Liechtenstein
New Hebrides
Panama
Switzerland
United States

10. *Trusts*

SETTLEMENTS
Bahamas
Bermuda
British Virgin Islands
Cayman
Cook Islands
Cyprus
Gibraltar
Guernsey
Hong Kong
Isle of Man
Jersey
Liechtenstein
Monaco
Nauru
New Hebrides
Panama
Turks and Caicos

UNIT TRUSTS
Bahamas
Bermuda
British Virgin Islands
Barbados
Cayman
Guernsey
Hong Kong
Isle of Man
Jersey
Nauru
Turks and Caicos

MUTUAL FUNDS
British Virgin Islands
Cook Islands
Guernsey
Isle of Man
Jersey
Luxembourg
Netherlands Antilles
Nauru
Turks and Caicos

11. *Bearer Shares*

Cayman
(Exempted Company)
Cook Islands
Gibraltar
Liberia
Liechtenstein
Luxembourg
Nauru
Netherlands (NV only)
Netherlands Antilles
Panama
Seychelles (Exempt Entities)
Switzerland
Turks and Caicos

(SHARE WARRANTS TO BEARER)
Barbados
Bahamas
British Virgin Islands
Hong Kong
Seychelles (Exempt Entities)
United Kingdom
Vanuatu

12. *Shares of No-Par Value*

Cayman (Exempted Company)
Cook Islands
Liberia
Liechtenstein
Luxembourg
Panama
Turks and Caicos
Vanuatu (unlimited company)

13. *Names*

Cayman
  Exempted Company: need not contain 'Ltd'

Cook Islands
  may end: Limited, Ltd, Incorporated, Inc., Corporation Corp.

Liberia
  may end: Limited, Limitada, Société Anonyme, Société par actions, Sociedad Anònima, Aktiengesellschaft, Corp., Inc., Ltd, Ltda, S.A., A.G.

Panama
  may end: Sociedad Anònima, S.A., Corp., Inc., – but not Ltd or Limited

Seychelles
  may end: Ltd, Inc., Corp.

Turks and Caicos
  Exempted Company: need not contain 'Ltd'

14. *Stepping Stones*

Canada
Denmark
Germany
Luxembourg
Netherlands
United Kingdom

15. *Management and Control*

Belgium
Denmark
France
Germany
Gibraltar
Luxembourg
Monaco
Netherlands
Panama
Switzerland
United States

16. *Administrative Offices*

Andorra
Belgium
France
Greece
Guernsey
Jersey
Liechtenstein
Luxembourg
Hong Kong
Isle of Man
Monaco
Panama
Singapore
Switzerland
United Kingdom
United States

17. *Emigration*

NO INCOME TAX ON INDIVIDUALS
Andorra
Antigua
Bahamas
Monaco

TERRITORIAL BASIS
Austria
Costa Rica
Hong Kong
Israel
Malta
Mexico
South Africa
Sri Lanka

EXEMPTIONS
Republic of Ireland
Sri Lanka

LOW TAX
British Virgin Islands
Guernsey
Isle of Man
Jersey
Switzerland

REMITTANCE BASIS
British Virgin Islands
Cyprus
Gibraltar
Republic of Ireland
Malaysia
Singapore
United Kingdom

18. *Foreigners able to own land*

Bahamas
Bermuda
British Virgin Islands
Costa Rica
Gibraltar
Guernsey
Hong Kong
Isle of Man
Jersey
Luxembourg
Panama
Turks and Caicos
United Kingdom

19. *Numbered Accounts*

Andorra
Austria
Luxembourg
Nauru
Panama
Switzerland

APPENDIX 2

Company Tax in Switzerland

The system of company taxation in Switzerland is by no means easy for a foreigner to grasp: three taxes are levied by the Federal Government and taxes are also levied by the Cantonal and municipal authorities.

To begin with the three Federal taxes: first, there is the Federal tax on corporate profits, at rates varying between 3.63 and 9.8 per cent. The rate varies in accordance with the ratio which the net profits of the company bear to its capital and reserves (or net worth), and the maximum rate of 9.8 per cent is applicable to a company whose profits are equal to or greater than just over 23 per cent of its net worth. Secondly, there is a Federal capital tax of 0.0825 per cent, which is payable on the capital and reserves of the company. And thirdly, there is the Federal anticipatory tax, which is essentially a withholding tax of 35 per cent levied on all distributions, whether by way of dividend or proceeds of liquidation, and which is levied also on interest paid on Swiss bonds and Swiss bank accounts (though not levied on commercial interest or on royalties).

The only major statutory exemption which is available at Federal level is the holding company or substantial participation exemption. This applies to a Swiss company which holds participations in other Swiss or foreign companies amounting to not less than 20 per cent of their capital in each case, or having in each case a market value in excess of two million Swiss francs. Where this exemption applies, the Federal tax on net profit is reduced in the proportion that the income from those participations bears to the total gross income of the company: if all the company's income is derived from qualifying participations, no Federal tax on net profits is payable.

Cantonal and communal taxes (the communal tax being generally calculated as a fraction of the Cantonal rate) represent the largest part of the tax liability both of individuals and of corporations in Switzerland. The normal rates of Cantonal tax on corporate profits rise to between roughly 30 and 38 per cent, and again the rate is calculated by reference to the ratio between the net profits of the company and its net worth. However, both the basic rates and the special tax concessions which are available vary significantly between each of the twenty five separate Cantonal taxing authorities: in considering the location of a branch or subsidiary for an activity in Switzerland, it pays to 'shop around' between Cantons.

There is some pressure from the Federal Government towards harmonisation of Cantonal tax practice. This would essentially mean the introduction of uniform rules of assessment, broadly comparable rates of tax and the restriction or elimination of present fiscal incentives. But while this may be inevitable in the long term, it is not yet within sight. While the Cantons continue to pursue autonomous, though not dissimilar, taxing policies, the privileges which are available vary greatly between Cantons and are in many cases negotiable with the appropriate tax authorities. These privileges include complete exoneration from Cantonal and communal taxes on foreign-source income, taxation of foreign-source income at special low Cantonal and communal rates, taxation at normal rates of a part only of the foreign income, and taxation at normal rates on a theoretical income calculated by reference to the overhead expenses of the company incurred in Switzerland or by reference to its total payroll. In considering the privileges granted by the Canton and municipalities, one must always bear in mind that these do not offset the company's liability to Federal taxes, of which much the most serious – in the long term – may be the distribution tax at the rate of 35 per cent (unless reduced by treaty).

All Cantons provide for a reduction of or even exemption from tax on dividend income, where the company qualifies as a holding company. Here the test is similar, but not identical, to that applied under the Federal tax rules mentioned above. The majority of Cantons offer a statutory concession known as the 'domiciliary' status and this applies to companies which maintain a registered office in Switzerland, but which have no commercial activity within the country and, generally, no permanent office staff, although certain Cantons (including Fribourg, Neuchatel and Valais) allow a company to maintain a small office staff and still qualify for the domiciliary privilege. Such a company would typically act as a European sales company for a group, or as a licensing or finance company, and in consequence of the domiciliary tax privilege it would, in a Canton such as Fribourg or Zug (which are two of the Cantons most favoured for this type of operation), be totally exempt from any Cantonal or municipal tax on its foreign income. Only a small Cantonal capital tax, not exceeding a rate typically between 0.1 and 0.5 per cent of the capital and reserves of the company, would be payable, and thus in effect such a company would be liable only to the Federal tax on net profits. For example, in the Canton of Vaud, companies which are foreign-controlled and whose commercial and industrial activities lie principally or exclusively outside Switzerland are regarded as domiciliary companies, and there special tax rules apply under which the company will pay Cantonal and communal taxes amounting together to 28 per cent on only 20 per cent of its net foreign profits, which gives an effective tax rate of 5.6 per cent.

Where a company's business activity necessitates an administrative office with personnel in significant numbers, or where the company engages in business in Switzerland and thus generates income from Swiss sources, the domiciliary privilege will not apply. In such a case the appropriate tax status is that known as a 'mixed' company. This is a status which is granted in a number of Cantons, including (among others) Zug, Geneva, Vaud, Valais and Zurich. Under this tax status the company will generally be taxed at the ordinary Cantonal rate of 30 to 38 per cent on its Swiss-source income and will be granted a special concessionary rate for its foreign-source income. For example, a company domiciled in Geneva will pay Cantonal tax on its Swiss-source income at ordinary rates of up to 35.7 per cent but on its foreign-source income at only 9 per cent. In the Canton of Vaud, Swiss-source income will be taxable at rates of up to 28 per cent, while the foreign-source income may be taxed only to the extent of 20 per cent of that income at the same 28 per cent rate – that is, at 5.6 per cent. Such a company – in either Canton – would typically be the kind of European sales company which requires substantial local personnel. Similar rulings are also available for Swiss branch offices of foreign companies.

There is also a special status for Swiss companies which render finance, marketing, public relations or other services to related companies situated outside Switzerland. Such a company may often be a simple domiciliary company, but if it requires more extensive administrative facilities and local personnel than would be permitted under the domiciliary tax status, certain Cantons will offer it a special tax arrangement. Companies benefiting from such arrangements are known as 'service' or 'auxiliary' companies. With a company of this kind, it may be difficult to determine its true profits, since the price charged for the services rendered to the foreign affiliated companies will not be accepted as being arrived at on an arm's-length basis for Swiss tax purposes. Cantons differ as to whether they will accept the book profits or whether they wish to make adjustments. Some Cantons require a minimum profit of 10 to 20 per cent of overhead expenses to be declared, and the Federal tax administration has issued a circular to all the Cantonal tax administrations, which effectively requires that a company carrying on such an activity for affiliated companies should report income similar to that which an independent company would have realised. The circular also contains guidelines to the effect that the taxable profit should not be less than 10 per cent of the expenses of the Swiss-based company, or one-sixth of its total payroll, together with taxable royalty and investment income.

Many Cantons have special provisions relating to the taxation of such companies, and other Cantons which do not have any specific statutory concessions will generally listen to any representations which may be made on behalf of a company intending to qualify as a service company. One of the features of the Swiss tax scene is that the Cantonal tax authorities are very approachable: they are prepared to listen to what a company wishes to do, and may issue a special tax ruling to cover the particular case.

One has to bear in mind the continuing difficulties of obtaining permits for foreign personnel. But the Swiss authorities have an essentially pragmatic approach to the question and are still prepared to grant favourable consideration to new businesses which wish to establish themselves in Switzerland, particularly if that business can be easily integrated into what is essentially a service economy in Switzerland, and if at the same time the new business will both generate employment for Swiss clerical and managerial personnel and make a significant contribution to the local revenue. Switzerland does not offer any tax concessions to foreign employees. On the other hand, the total of the normal Federal, Cantonal and municipal taxes are not high by general European standards: for example, a married man living in Zurich, having a total income of 100,000 Swiss francs, will pay tax at an average of 27 per cent. Marginal rates do not generally exceed 40 per cent. On top of the personal income tax, there is a social security levy which also goes towards pension contributions, levied at a flat rate of 10 per cent on all salaries, of which one-half is payable by the employee and the other half by the employer.

Switzerland has a limited use as a Stepping Stone country: although it is party to a large number of tax treaties, the 1962 Decree limits the extent to which deductions may be made against passive (but not business) income which enjoys the benefit of a treaty. In addition, at least 25 per cent of such treaty privileged income must be distributed by the Swiss corporate recipient in the form of a dividend. But by taking advantage of such deductions as are permitted, complying with the minimum distribution requirement and accumulating the residue of the income, a Swiss domiciliary company may reduce the immediate tax on, for example, patent royalties to something below 14 per cent.

APPENDIX 3

Cayman Islands: The Trusts Law (Revised), Part V

Exempted Trusts

68. The Governor shall appoint such person as he may from time to time think fit to be the Registrar of Trusts for the purpose of registering, controlling and otherwise dealing with exempted trusts in accordance with the provisions of this Part.

69. (1) Where the Registrar of Trusts is satisfied that the beneficiaries under any trust do not and are not likely to include any person at any time resident or domiciled in the Islands (other than any object of a charitable trust or power) he may, upon application made by the trustees at any time, register such trust as an exempted trust.
(2) After the Registrar of Trusts has registered a trust as an exempted trust, it shall not cease to be an exempted trust by reason of the fact that any beneficiary is at any time resident or domiciled in the Islands but any such beneficiary shall nevertheless be subject to the provisions of subsection (3) of section 76.
(3) The Registrar of Trusts may if he thinks fit decline to approve for registration or to register any trust without giving any reason for so declining.
(4) The Registrar of Trusts may if he thinks fit (but subject to section 79) decline to consider any application under this section or any submission under section 77 unless the applicant procure from such of the beneficiaries then in existence and ascertained as the Registrar of Trusts may specify a declaration that he is not and does not intend to become resident or domiciled in the Islands.

70. Upon the registration of any trust as an exempted trust (or if the registration of a trust takes effect under section 77 then upon receipt of any draft document as there mentioned) the Registrar of Trusts shall issue to the trustees thereof a certificate to that effect and the Trustees shall pay to the Registrar of Trusts a registration fee of $200.

71. (1) Trustees making application to the Registrar of Trusts for the registration of any trust under this Part shall lodge with the Registrar of Trusts all and any documents containing or recording the

trusts powers and provisions thereof together with a copy of such documents.

(2) The Registrar shall retain in each case every such document and shall (if such be the case) certify that the copy is a true copy thereof and shall return the certified copy to the trustees.

72. (1) The trustees shall from time to time furnish the Registrar of Trusts with such accounts minutes and information relating to the trust as the Registrar may from time to time require.

(2) The Registrar of Trusts shall keep and maintain a file containing every document lodged under the provisions of section 71 together with all accounts minutes and letters or other documents containing information furnished to him which shall be open to inspection by any trustee of the trust or any person specifically so authorised by the provisions of the trust and by the Registrar of Trusts and shall not be open to inspection by any other person but a person entitled to inspection of the file shall be entitled to take copies of the contents thereof and in the course of any proceedings to produce or (as the case may be) require the Registrar of Trusts to produce the file and the contents thereof in evidence and the same shall be admissible as *prima facie* evidence of the facts and matters therein appearing.

73. In March of each year the trustees of every exempted trust shall pay to the revenues of the Islands an annual fee of $100 or such lesser sum as the income of the trust shall amount to for the previous calendar year.

74. Where the trustees of any exempted trust fail to comply with the provisions of section 72 or section 73 and receive written notice to this effect from the Registrar of Trusts then if the provisions of sections 72 and 73 shall not have been complied with within 28 days (or such further period as the Registrar of Trusts may allow) of the receipt of such notice by the trustees, the Court may upon application made by the Registrar of Trusts remove any one or more of the trustees and appoint a trustee or trustees in his or their place and generally make such order (including any order as to costs and as to payment and as to reinbursement of any fee and of any costs) as the Court may think fit.

75. Whoever knowingly furnishes to the Registrar of Trusts any false declaration document account minute or information or permits the same to be so furnished knowing it to be false is guilty of an offence, and liable on summary conviction to imprisonment for a term not exceeding three months or to a fine in lieu of or in addition to such imprisonment as aforesaid not exceeding $1,000.

76. (1) It is lawful for the Governor in Council to give an undertaking to the trustees of an exempted trust who make application therefor that no law which is hereafter enacted in the Islands imposing any tax or duty to be levied on income or on capital assets, gains or appreciation or any

tax in the nature of estate duty or inheritance tax shall apply to any property comprised in or any income arising under such exempted trust or to the trustees or the beneficiaries thereof in respect of any such property or income.

(2) Any such undertaking as aforesaid may be for any period not exceeding 50 years from the date of the creating of the exempted trust and may be in such form as the Governor in Council shall determine.

(3) Notwithstanding the foregoing provisions of this section and anything contained in any such undertaking a beneficiary who is at any time resident or domiciled in the Islands shall be liable in and in respect of such time to all and any tax and duty as if such undertaking had never been given and nothing in this section shall be construed as exempting any other person resident or domiciled in the Islands from the provisions of any Law imposing any tax or duty referred to in this Law.

77. Any person intending to create any trust (otherwise than by will or codicil), or any person on his behalf, may submit to the Registrar of Trusts a draft of any document expressed to contain or record the trust powers and provisions thereof and any person intending to be a trustee thereof may apply to the Governor for an undertaking in accordance with section 76 whereupon the Registrar (on being satisfied in accordance with section 69) may approve the same for registration and the Governor shall be at liberty to give such undertaking as is mentioned in section 76 and such registration and undertaking shall take effect and shall take effect only on the creation of the trust in accordance with such draft within 28 days (or such further period as the Registrar of Trusts may allow) of such approval or the giving of such undertaking (whichever shall later occur) and the trustees shall nevertheless forthwith lodge with the Registrar the documents creating the trust in accordance with the provisions of section 71.

78. Where the registration of a trust as an exempted trust takes effect in accordance with section 77 and the trust instrument so provides, the perpetuity period applicable to any disposition made by such instrument under the rule against perpetuities, instead of being of any other duration, shall be of a duration equal to such number of years not exceeding 100 as is therein specified in that behalf.

79. (1) Subsection (4) of section 69 shall not apply upon any submission to the Registrar of Trusts in accordance with section 77 where the settler (or any person on his behalf) shall in writing so request and where under the trusts powers and provisions of the draft submitted income or capital (other than income or capital applicable for any charitable purpose) is to any extent liable to be or capable of being transferred paid applied or appointed to or for the benefit of one or more beneficiaries in consequence of the exercise (whether with or without the consent of any person) of any discretion conferred on any person (not

being a discretion conferred on any beneficiary) but if the Registrar of Trusts shall approve the same and the settler shall create a trust in accordance therewith and within the time specified in section 77 the following provisions of this section shall apply to such trust.

(2) Where but for the provisions of subsection (3) any right or remedy would be vested in any one or more of the beneficiaries thereunder the same shall be vested in and shall be exercisable by the Registrar of Trusts and any sum or sums recovered by the Registrar of Trusts shall be paid to the trustees, and the Registrar of Trusts in relation to the exercise of the said rights and remedies and the payments of sums recovered pursuant thereto shall be answerable to the Governor in Council as *parens patriae* and to no other person.

(3) No beneficiary shall in relation to the trust fund or any income thereof, at any time have any right or remedy at law or in equity against the Crown, the Governor, the Registrar of Trusts or the trustees or any servant or agent of any of them and in particular (but without prejudice to the generality of the foregoing) –

(*a*) no beneficiary shall be entitled to require any money or property subject to the trust any income or capital of the trust fund to be paid transferred appropriated applied or appointed in any way whatsoever,

(*b*) no beneficiary shall be entitled to be taken into consideration by the trustees or the Registrar of Trusts or to require the trustees or Registrar of Trusts to take him into consideration in or about the exercise of any power discretion or duty conferred upon them or any of them,

(*c*) no beneficiary shall have any rights or remedies in connection with or in relation to the administration of the trust fund, and accordingly no beneficiary shall be entitled to inspect any accounts minutes or documents relating to the trust,

(*d*) no action brought by or at the suit of any beneficiary (whether alone or jointly with any other person) against any trustee or the Registrar of Trusts or in respect of the trust fund in any manner whatsoever shall be entertained by the Court.

(*e*) In this subsection the expression 'trustee' includes any person in whom under or by virtue of the terms of the trust there is vested (whether in a fiduciary capacity or not) any power or duty whatsoever.

(4) The trustees or any of them or the Registrar of Trusts shall at any time and from time to time be at liberty to apply to the Court in and about any matter affecting the trust and the Court shall (subject to subsection (5)) give such directions and make such order (including any order as to costs) as may be just, and in particular and without prejudice to the generality of the foregoing the trustees or any of them are at liberty to proceed against any trustee or person who has been a trustee of the trust in respect of any breach of that trust.

(5) Nothing in Part IV of this Law applies to a trust exempted by this section.

80. The trustees of any exempted trust shall be entitled (except where the Court may in any case otherwise order) to be reimbursed out of the trust fund any fee payable or other expense incurred by them under this Part.

81. If the Registrar of Trusts is satisfied that no property remains subject to the trusts powers or provisions thereof he shall so certify whereupon the provisions of this Part shall cease to apply to such trust or any former trustees thereof and the file relating to such trust and its contents shall be destroyed.

82. (1) In this Part unless the context otherwise requires –

beneficiary means any person interested under a trust (whether or not he is the principal beneficiary and notwithstanding that his interest is liable to be affected or defeated by any exercise of any power vested in any person) and a person is deemed to be interested under a trust if any capital or income comprised in the trust is liable to be or capable of being transferred paid applied or appointed to him or for his benefit either pursuant to the terms of the trust or in consequence of an exercise of any power or discretion conferred on any person by such terms but does not include any person by reason only that he is remunerated or indemnified as a trustee or as the servant of the agent of a trustee;

'trust' means any settlement declaration of trust or other similar disposition created *inter vivos* or by will (including codicil) and taking effect under the law in force in the Islands.

(2) The provisions of this Part shall apply in relation to a disposition made otherwise than by an instrument as if the disposition had been contained in an instrument taking effect when the disposition was made.
(3) Parts I, II, III and VI and all the rules of law and equity shall (subject to subsection (5) of section 79) apply to every exempted trust as to any other trust save as expressly provided in this Part.

APPENDIX 4

Monaco: Law No. 214 of 1936

(Modifying Law No. 207 of 12th July 1935, regarding trusts, (27th February 1936))

Louis II by the Grace of God Sovereign Prince of Monaco has sanctioned and hereby sanctions the Law of which the text follows which the National Council has adopted at its audience of 6th February, 1936.

Title I – Constitution of Trusts – Reglementation

Article 1

Persons who by virtue of their personal law have the faculty of arranging the destination of their assets either in their lifetime or after their death by adopting a form of trust may use the same within the territory of the Principality with the co-operation and support of local institutions.

Article 2

The constitution of the Trust must be made, under pain of nullity, by deed in authentic (notarial) form supported by an attestation that (the terms of) the deed are in conformity with the foreign law under the authority of which it is placed. This attestation must be given by a qualified lawyer.
The qualification is evidenced by the inscription on a list drawn up and maintained by the First President of the Court of Appeal on the proposal of the Procurator General.
Are inscribed on this list as of right, on demand, for England any Solicitor of the Supreme Court of Judicature, for America any Attorney-at-Law.

Article 3

Are alone able to act as Trustees such normal persons (corporations) and, if necessary, as co-Trustees such physical persons selected in either case from a list specially drawn up and maintained by the First President of the Court of Appeal on the proposal of the Procurator General.
Monegasque Law is alone competent to the exclusion of the foreign law for the determination and designation of the Trustees who therefore do not come within the terms of the attestation provided for on Article 2, paragraph 1 above.
Exceptionally the co-Trustee may in conformity with the foreign law

selected be freely designated by the founder of the trust without being inscribed on the list provided by Article 2 but on condition that he acts only for this one trust and in conformity with the foreign law selected.

Article 4

The transfer within the Principality of a trust created outside is carried out in the same manner as the constitution of a trust as provided in the foregoing Articles. This transfer is permitted for any person who on the date of the constitution (of the trust) was a foreign national even though he may have subsequently changed his nationality even to that of Monegasque.

The creation in Monaco in conformity with the present law of a new trust destined to replace a trust previously constituted outside will be considered as regards the present Article as the equivalent of a transfer.

Article 5

All contestations relating either to the constitution or the transfer or to the functioning of trusts within the Principality shall be submitted to the Monegasque Courts who shall here apply in conformity with the present law the provisions of the foreign law without being bound by considerations of Monegasque public order.

Article 6

The only taxes arising on the creation, the transfer and the functioning of trusts are the registration duties referred to in Title II as follows.

Title II – Fiscal Provisions

Article 7

The deeds creating or transferring trusts within the Principality are subject to proportional registration duties which vary according to the number of beneficiaries succeeding in the trust and which are fixed at the following rates –

One Beneficiary	1,30 %
Two Beneficiaries	1,50 %
More than two Beneficiaries	1,70 %

The duty is converted into an annual tax of 0,20 % if the parties make such application in the deed constituting the trust.

The duty or tax is collected to the exclusion of all gift taxes or death duties.

In both cases, the tax is liquidated on the total amount of the value of the estate invested in the trust, with the exception of Monegasque securities referred to in Article 8.

For securities, the capital adopted for the liquidation of the duty is determined by the middle Stock Exchange price on the date of the death of the person constituting the trust, if it is a testamentary trust.

This middle price is the London Stock Exchange price when the trust is constituted by a person of English nationality and that of the New York Stock Exchange when the trust is constituted by persons of any other nationality.

For securities not quoted on the Stock Exchange, the capital is determined on the value estimated by the trustee without deduction of charges.

The tax of 0,20 % is payable in advance and by annuities. These annuities must be paid, the first at the time of registration of the deed, and subsequently, within the first ten days of the month of January each year, under penalty of a fine equal to one fourth of the tax due.

The trustees are personally responsible for the payment of the annuities with the exception of the first.

Article 8

The capital of the trusts represented by Monegasque securities is subject to a reduced proportional duty and fixed in the following manner taking into account the number of the beneficiaries succeeding in the trust –

One Beneficiary	0,05 %
Two Beneficiaries...	0,25 %
More than two Beneficiaries	0,45 %

This duty, which is paid at the time of the registration of the deed constituting the trust, takes the place of any other gift taxes or death duties.

It is liquidated under the conditions set down in the preceding Article for foreign securities.

Article 9

The duties and taxes mentioned above are collected in conformity with the dispositions of the Sovereign Ordinance of 29th April, 1928, in so far as these dispositions are not modified by the present law.

APPENDIX 5

Gibraltar: Companies (Taxation and Concessions) Ordinance 1983

1. This Ordinance may be cited as the Companies (Taxation and Concessions) Ordinance, 1983.

2. (1) In this Ordinance, unless the context otherwise requires, –

'exempt company' means a company in respect of which there is for the time being in force an exemption certificate issued under section 5 by the Financial and Development Secretary;

'Gibraltarian' means a person registered as a Gibraltarian under the Gibraltarian Status Ordinance, or a person who is entitled to be so registered under that Ordinance, but does not mean –

(*a*) a person in respect of whom there is in force an order of the Financial and Development Secretary under section 16 that such person shall not be treated as a Gibraltarian for the purposes of this Ordinance; or

(*b*) an exempt company;

'ordinarily resident in Gibraltar' has the same meaning as it has for purposes of the Income Tax Ordinance;

'resident of Gibraltar' includes –

(*a*) a person ordinarily resident in Gibraltar; or

(*b*) a company, not ordinarily resident in Gibraltar, in whose shares (other than shares of a class quoted on a recognised stock exchange) any Gibraltarian or resident of Gibraltar is interested;

but does not include –

(i) a person in respect of whom there is in force an order of the Financial and Development Secretary under section 16 that such person shall not be treated as resident or ordinarily resident in Gibraltar; or

(ii) an exempt company (whether or not ordinarily resident in Gibraltar);

'share' means a share in the share capital of a company, and also means stock except where a distinction between stock and shares is expressed or implied.

(2) For the purposes of this Ordinance, a person shall be deemed to be interested in a share, loan or debenture if –

(*a*) he holds any interest therein (other than as a bare nominee or trustee thereof) either directly or indirectly or through a company or series of companies and whether such interest is equitable, legal or contractual; or

(*b*) by reason of any agreement or arrangement with any other person he has the right to acquire an interest therein as herein defined or the power to enjoy a dividend or other benefit thereof.

(3) Notwithstanding subsection (2), a person shall not be deemed to be interested in a share, loan or debenture by reason of his holding the same or any interest therein acting in a representative or fiduciary capacity only, even though he may be entitled to remuneration for so acting or may have a charge or lien thereon for such remuneration.

3. For the purposes of this Ordinance, a company shall be eligible to be an exempt company if, but only if, all of the following requirements are fulfilled in respect of it:

(*a*) it is registered in Gibraltar under the Companies Ordinance:

(*b*) the paid-up share capital of the company is not less than £100, or, where the share capital is expressed in any other currency, is not less than an amount equivalent to £100 at the ruling rate of exchange in the London foreign exchange market:

(*c*) the company does not, without the approval of the Financial and Development Secretary, carry on or transact any trade or business in Gibraltar, unless that trade or business is such that all receipts and income arising from it in the ordinary course of the trade or business arise either outside Gibraltar or from dealings with other exempt companies and originate from persons other than Gibraltarians or residents of Gibraltar; for which purpose only, the holding and managing of investments or property shall be treated as a trade or business:

Provided always that the company may in Gibraltar buy, sell, deal in, or hold and manage investments and property outside Gibraltar, or shares or debentures or other interests in other exempt companies, or debts or other choses in action owed or created by or enforceable against persons other than Gibraltarians or residents of Gibraltar, and may in Gibraltar promote services to be performed for other exempt companies, or services to be performed outside Gibraltar by and for persons other than Gibraltarians or residents of Gibraltar, without contravening this requirement:

(*d*) the company –

(i) where it is not registered under Part IX of the Companies Ordinance, does not keep and is prohibited by its memorandum or articles of association from keeping any register of shares outside Gibraltar;

and

(ii) where it is registered under Part IX of that Ordinance, and is not a public company whose shares are quoted in a manner approved by the Financial and Development Secretary, keeps in Gibraltar a certified true copy of every share register kept by the company outside Gibraltar:

(*e*) no Gibraltarian or resident of Gibraltar is interested in any of its shares, other than as a shareholder in a public company –

(i) that is registered under a law, of a country other than Gibraltar, relating to the registration or incorporation of bodies corporate; and

(ii) the shares of which are quoted on a recognised stock exchange:

(*f*) the company, where it is registered under Part IX of the Companies Ordinance, is not of a class for the time being prescribed for the purposes of this paragraph.

4. Any person wishing to acquire for an existing company or for a company to be formed under the Companies Ordinance the status of an exempt company may make application in writing in the prescribed form to the Financial and Development Secretary for the grant of an exemption certificate under this Ordinance.

5. (1) The Financial and Development Secretary, where he is satisfied that a company complies with the requirements of section 3, may in his absolute discretion register such company as an exempt company and issue under his hand an exemption certificate subject to such conditions and restrictions as he may think fit, and the company shall be an exempt company as from such date as may be stated in the certificate.

(2) Subject to sections 6 and 15, an exemption certificate shall remain in force for a period of 25 years after the date so stated in it.

(3) The Financial and Development Secretary may at any time demand from any person such information and evidence in support thereof as he thinks fit to ensure compliance with all or any of the provisions and requirements of this Ordinance, including any conditions and restrictions imposed by the exemption certificate.

(4) A person who without lawful excuse fails to give such information or supply such evidence is guilty of an offence and shall be liable on summary conviction to a fine of £500.

6. Subject to section 15, an exempt company shall cease to be an exempt company if –

(*a*) the company reduces its nominal share capital to a sum below the amount specified in section 3 (*b*) in respect of that company; or (*b*) the company alters its memorandum or articles of association without the prior consent in writing of the Financial and Development Secretary; or

(*c*) the company makes or gives effect (by registration or otherwise) to any dealing or purported dealing with its shares contrary to section 7, or section 11 (2) is contravened in respect of the commany; or

(*d*) any of the requirements that apply to the company under section 3 (other than paragraph (*f*)) ceases to be fulfilled in respect of the company; or

(*e*) the company makes default in payment of any instalment of annual tax payable by it after the day on which such instalment has been under section 10 (3) become payable; or

(*f*) the company makes default in complying with any condition or restriction imposed by the exemption certificate; or

(*g*) the company or any of its directors or (except in the case of a public company) any of its shareholders is convicted of an offence under section 5 (4) or section 17.

7. (1) Where an exempt company is not a public company whose shares are quoted in a manner approved by the Financial and Development Secretary –

(*a*) the exempt company shall not without the approval of the Financial and Development Secretary allot or issue any of its shares; and

(*b*) no person holding any shares in the company or any interest therein shall transfer or attempt to transfer or sell or enter into any legally binding commitment to sell such shares, without first submitting to the Financial and Development Secretary the prescribed particulars, in respect of the proposed transferee or purchaser or beneficiary of the shares or interest therein, and obtaining the approval in writing of the Financial and Development Secretary for the proposed transaction –

but in the case of an exempt company –

(i) the shares of which are registered in the names of trustees; and

(ii) which does not in the course of its trade or business accept deposits of money or other assets from the public or from any section of the public –

nothing in this subsection shall apply to the acquisition (by transfer or sale or any other means) of an interest by a new or substituted beneficiary under the trust administered by those trustees unless the Financial and Development Secretary in any particular case so directs where he is apprehensive that a person has acquired or is about to acquire an interest, being a person who would not have been acceptable to the Financial and Development Secretary as a shareholder on the application by the company under section 4 for registration as anexempt company.

(2) Unless otherwise directed by the Financial and Development Secretary, where an exempt company is a public company whose shares are quoted in a manner approved by the Financial and Development Secretary, no person shall issue any share or register the transfer of any share unless there is delivered to the person issuing the share or registering the transfer a statutory declaration signed by the allottee or transferee of the share stating that no Gibraltarian or resident of Gibraltar thereby acquires an interest in the share or transfer.

(3) Any dealing with a share contrary to this section shall be null and void.

8. (1) Subject to subsections (2), (3) and (4), but notwithstanding the provisions of the Income Tax Ordinance, while an exemption certificate remains in force in respect of an exempt company, it shall enjoy the following benefits:

(*a*) no tax under the Income Tax Ordinance shall be charged on or payable on the profits of the company; and

(*b*) no tax under that Ordinance shall be charged on or payable on any dividend, interest, director's fee, annual payment or other sum payable by the company to any person who is not either a Gibraltarian or a resident of Gibraltar; and

(*c*) the company shall be under no liability to deduct tax from the amount of any dividend, interest, fee, annual payment or other sum specified in paragraph (*b*); and

(*d*) neither of sections 13 and 14 of the Income Tax Ordinance shall apply to the company.

(2) An exempt company shall be liable to tax under the Income Tax Ordinance in respect of income arising from any trade or business or the holding of any investments or property in respect of which the approval of the Financial and Development Secretary is required under section 3 (*c*) in the same manner as if it were not an exempt company and the provisions of section 26 of the Income Tax Ordinance relating to the deduction of tax on dividends shall apply to an exempt company to the extent of any tax payable pursuant to this section.

(3) The provisions of section 27 of the Income Tax Ordinance relating to the deduction of tax from interest paid by certain companies shall apply to an exempt company in respect of any mortgage, or debenture interest or interest on any loan advanced to the company where the interest is payable to a Gibraltarian or a resident of Gibraltar or is interest on principal money secured upon any immovable property situate in Gibraltar, and the company shall account for such tax to the Commissioner of Income Tax under the provisions of that Ordinance.

(4) Nothing in this section shall exempt any rent or other periodical sum payable in respect of, or payable for the use or occupation of, or charged on, immovable property situate in Gibraltar (whether or not

payable to a Gibraltarian or a resident of Gibraltar) from tax under the Income Tax Ordinance.

9. (1) Subject to subsection (2), but notwithstanding the provisions of the Estate Duties Ordinance –

(*a*) all shares in, loans made to, debentures held in and policies of life assurance issued by an exempt company shall be exempt from estate duty; and

(*b*) the value of the shares, loans, debentures and policies specified in paragraph (*a*) shall not be taken into account or aggregated with any other property for the purpose of determining the rate at which estate duty is payable on any other property.

(2) Subsection (1) shall not apply to –

(*a*) any loan or debenture –

(i) in which any Gibraltarian or resident of Gibraltar is interested; or

(ii) which is secured upon any immovable property situated in Gibraltar; or

(*b*) any policy of life assurance issued on the life of any Gibraltarian or resident of Gibraltar.

(3) Notwithstanding the provisions of the Stamp Duties Ordinance –

(*a*) no stamp duty shall be payable on the issue of any policy of life assurance that is, by virtue of section 9, exempt from estate duty; and

(*b*) no stamp duty shall be payable on any annuity payable by an exempt company; and

(*c*) no stamp duty shall be payable on any dealings by way of sale, mortgage or other means with any such policy or annuity.

10. (1) Subject to subsections (2) and (4), there shall be payable by every exempt company in respect of every year of assessment during which it continues to be an exempt company and rateable on a monthly basis for every month or part thereof for which it shall continue to be an exempt company an annual tax, at the following rate:

(*a*) in the case of an exempt company that is ordinarily resident in Gibraltar, but is not registered under Part IX of the Companies Ordinance, £225 per annum:

(*b*) in the case of an exempt company that is not ordinarily resident in Gibraltar, and is not registered under Part IX of the Companies Ordinance, £200 per annum;

(*c*) in the case of a company that is registered under Part IX of the Companies Ordinance, £500 per annum.

(2) Notwithstanding subsection (1) of this section, where the activities of an exempt company are limited solely and exclusively to the holding of securities in respect of which income tax has been deducted at the

source and in respect of which relief would be granted from tax in Gibraltar under section 30 of the Income Tax Ordinance if the company had not been an exempt company, the annual tax payable by that company shall be payable at half the rate applicable to the company under subsection (1) of this section.

(3) Annual tax shall be payable to the Accountant General in half yearly instalments, the first instalment of which shall be payable within thirty days of the issue of the exemption certificate for so much of the half year ending on the 30th day of September or the 31st day of March, as the case may be, as may remain unexpired, and the subsequent instalments of which shall be payable in advance on the 1st day of April and the 1st day of October in each year of assessment.

(4) An exempt company ordinarily resident in Gibraltar for the purposes of the Income Tax Ordinance may by notice in writing addressed to the Financial and Development Secretary and received by him not later than the end of any year of assessment, elect to pay income tax under the provisions of the Income Tax Ordinance for the time being in force, and in such case until the election so made is revoked by the company by subsequent notice in writing addressed to the Financial and Development Secretary –

(*a*) so much of subsection (3) of section 8 as provides that no tax under the Income Tax Ordinance shall be charged on or payable upon the profits of the company, or on any dividend payable by the company, and that the company shall not be liable to deduct tax from any such dividend, shall cease to have effect as from the beginning of that year of assessment (but without prejudice to the continued operation of the other provisions of the said subsection (3)); and

(*b*) annual tax shall be payable by the company at the same rates as if it were not so ordinarily resident (but only for the period after the notice of election is received); and

(*c*) annual tax paid by the company for any year of assessment during which the election is in force shall be treated for all tax purposes as on account of the tax payable by the company under the Income Tax Ordinance for that year of assessment.

(5) A revocation of an election under subsection (4) shall not take effect until the end of the year of assessment in which the notice or revocation is received.

(6) Where an election has been made under subsection (4) to pay income tax under the Income Tax Ordinance, annual tax shall be payable at the rate specified in paragraph (*b*) of that subsection notwithstanding that the amount of income tax payable is nil or is less than the amount of annual tax.

(7) Upon final settlement of the liability of an exempt company for annual tax and any tax under the Income Tax Ordinance for any year of assessment (including payment in full of any tax payable), the

Financial and Development Secretary shall, on application made by the company, certify in writing either that the company was or (as the case may be) that the company was not ordinarily resident in Gibraltar for the purposes of the Income Tax Ordinance during the whole or some part of the year of assessment (according to the basis on which the said liability was settled), and any certificate so given shall be conclusive as to the facts so certified.

(8) The provisions of sections 55 to 57 inclusive, 62, 64 and 65 of the Income Tax Ordinance (relating to appeals against assessments and to recovery, remission and repayment of tax) shall, subject to the provisions of this Ordinance, apply *mutatis mutandis* to annual tax as they apply to tax under the Income Tax Ordinance.

11. (1) Any exempt company, not being a public company registered under the Companies Ordinance, may issue bearer certificates or coupons (as defined in section 2 of the Exchange Control Ordinance) or convert its share capital to bearer certificates provided that –

(*a*) the bearer certificates and coupons remain deposited in Gibraltar or elsewhere with a bank on behalf of the persons approved by the Financial and Development Secretary as shareholders; and

(*b*) no other person has any interest in any such shares except as may be approved in writing by the Financial and Development Secretary.

(2) Except as provided in subsection (1), no exempt company may issue bearer certificates or coupons or convert its share capital to bearer certificates.

12. (1) A bank shall not part with possession of bearer certificates or coupons deposited with it under section 11 without the prior permission in writing of the Financial and Development Secretary which may be either general or special to any particular case.

(2) Except with the permission of the Financial and Development Secretary, a bank shall not do any act whereby it recognises or gives effect to the substitution of one person for another as the person from whom it receives instructions in relation to a certificate of title or coupon, unless there is produced to it the prescribed evidence that it is not by so doing giving effect to any transaction which is prohibited by this Ordinance.

(3) A bank that contravenes the provisions of this section shall be guilty of an offence and shall be liable on summary conviction to a fine of £1,000.

13. (1) A person or firm shall not be qualified for appointment as auditor of an exempt company unless he or it is approved by the Governor for the purposes of this section and is a member or is a firm whose partners are members of a body of accountants established in the United Kingdom and for the time being recognised for the purposes of the Companies Acts by the Department of Trade.

(2) The auditor shall, before the 30th day of June in every year, submit to the Commissioner of Income Tax a list of the full names of any resident of Gibraltar who has, during the period of a year ending on the 31st day of March, made any loan to the company and of the full names of any person other than a resident of Gibraltar who has, during the period of a year ending on the 31st day of March, made any loan to the company secured upon any immovable property situate in Gibraltar, and shall further give the following particulars in respect of any such loan, that is to say, the date and amount thereof and of any repayment or partial repayment thereof, the rate of interest and date when due and when paid with the amount of each payment.

(3) The auditor of an exempt company, being a public company whose shares are quoted in a manner approved by the Financial and Development Secretary under section 7, shall before the 30th day of April, in every year, submit a certificate to the Financial and Development Secretary containing a statement that the provisions of subsection (2) of section 7 have been complied with.

14. (1) Subject to the provisions of this section, the Financial and Development Secretary and every person having any official duty in the administration of this Ordinance shall regard and deal with all documents, information and declarations relating to the identity of the beneficial owners or persons interested in any shares, or bearer certificates or coupons issued under the provisions of this Ordinance as secret and confidential.

(2) Any person having possession of or control over any document, information or declaration relating to the identity of the beneficial owners of or persons interested in any share or bearer certificates or coupons issued under the provisions of this Ordinance (other than the person or all the persons to whose identity the document, information or declaration relates or some person thereunto authorised by him or them) who at any time communicates or attempts to communicate such information or anything contained in any such document or declaration to any person otherwise than for the purposes of this Ordinance or the Income Tax Ordinance or the Estate Duties Ordinance or the Exchange Control Ordinance or for the purposes of any criminal or civil proceedings in which such shares or bearer certificates or coupons are material shall be guilty of an offence and liable on summary conviction to a fine of £1,000.

(3) No person employed in carrying out the provisions of this Ordinance shall be required to produce in any court or before any authority or person for any purpose whatsoever any document or declaration made in pursuance of this Ordinance or to divulge or communicate to any court any matter or thing coming to his notice in the performance of his duties under this Ordinance except as may be necessary for the purpose of carrying into effect the provisions of this Ordinance or the Income Tax Ordinance or the Estate Duties

Ordinance or the Exchange Control Ordinance or for the purposes of any criminal or civil proceedings in which such document, declaration, matter or thing is material.

15. (1) In case of any such act or default by or in respect of an exempt company as is mentioned in paragraph (*a*) to (*g*) inclusive of section 6, the Financial and Development Secretary may in his discretion certify that the act or default was excusable and made or allowed without intent to defeat the provisions of this Ordinance, and if the Financial and Development Secretary so certifies the exempt company shall not cease to be an exempt company by reason only of that act or default; but subject thereto and without prejudice to the liability of any other person in respect of income tax or estate duty, a company ceasing to be an exempt company in consequence of any such act or default and every officer thereof who is knowingly responsible for the act or default without lawful excuse shall be jointly and severally liable for all taxes due from or deducted by the company consequent upon its ceasing to be an exempt company together with interest thereon at the rate of three *per centum per annum* from the date of the act or default.

(2) If the default was the failure to pay any annual tax, the Financial and Development Secretary shall not certify in accordance with the provisions of subsection (1) unless –

(*a*) a fee of £25 is paid for such certification; and
(*b*) all arrears of annual tax are paid:

Provided that in respect of all annual tax after the first instalment, the fee of £25 shall not be payable if the company has paid all arrears of annual tax within thirty days after the day on which such tax has become payable.

16. (1) The Financial and Development Secretary may by order declare that any person registered as a Gibraltarian under the Gibraltarian Status Ordinance or a person entitled to be so registered under that Ordinance, shall not, for the purposes of this Ordinance, be treated as a Gibraltarian.

(2) The Financial and Development Secretary may by order declare that any person ordinarily resident in Gibraltar for the purposes of the Income Tax Ordinance shall not, for the purposes of this Ordinance, be treated as resident or ordinarily resident in Gibraltar.

17. A person who without reasonable excuse gives any incorrect information, such information being required of him for the purpose of obtaining exemption for a company or otherwise carrying this Ordinance into effect, is guilty of an offence and shall be liable on summary conviction to a fine of £500 and double the amount of tax or duty which would have been chargeable if the information given had been correct or, if any such incorrect information is given wilfully and with intent to evade or to assist any other person in evading any tax or duty, to a fine

of £1,000 and treble the amount of such tax or duty, or to imprisonment for three years or to both such fine and imprisonment.

18. The Governor may from time to time make rules for all or any of the following purposes:

(*a*) providing for the returns to be submitted and the information to be furnished for the purpose of claiming exemption under this Ordinance;

(*b*) prescribing any matters required by this Ordinance to be prescribed;

(*c*) generally for giving effect to the purposes of this Ordinance.

19. (1) The Companies (Taxation and Concessions) Ordinance (in this section called 'the former Ordinance') is repealed.

(2) Every reference in every other enactment to the former Ordinance or to any of its provisions shall, unless the context otherwise requires, be construed as including a reference to this Ordinance or to the corresponding provision in this Ordinance.

(3) The repeal of the former Ordinance shall not affect any status, rights, or advantages held by any company or other person under that Ordinance immediately before its repeal, but the status, rights, and advantages shall from the commencement of this Ordinance be held in accordance with this Ordinance.

APPENDIX 6

Residence: A Case Study

Mr X lived in the United Kingdom – that is to say, he was resident, ordinarily resident and domiciled there for tax purposes. He was the sole proprietor of a U.K. company and its true guiding spirit. The company carried on a successful manufacturing business. It had no significant export business, but Mr X believed that similar enterprises could be established in other European countries – and perhaps elsewhere – and that so long as these enterprises were effectively controlled by him, his experience in manufacture and marketing would make them successful.

Mr X expressed a desire to emigrate from the United Kingdom, and to establish himself somewhere in continental Europe. It was not that he was conscious of having suffered any very grievous burden of tax in the past: the effect of capital allowances and stock relief had been that an expanding company of this kind was able to make profits virtually free of corporation tax, so long as the profits were not distributed to the shareholders (which in this case they were not). The salary which he drew from the company attracted tax at steeply progressive rates up to what had recently been 75 per cent, but he had kept his salary at a low level. He felt, however, that in the longer term his presence in the United Kingdom would prove a grave stumbling block in the way of the achievement of what he regarded as his main ambition – to be able to leave (or at least, be in a position to leave) to his son all the shares in his company, unencumbered by debt, when he died. He had built his company up from virtually nothing. He reckoned, leaving inflation out of account, that the company would at his death be worth, say, £8m. To provide for the capital transfer tax then payable would require a fund, outside the company, of £12m. How could that possibly be done?

It was with these thoughts that Mr X turned his mind to going to live somewhere else. He thought first of jurisdictions which do not impose these taxes. The Bahamas he judged too remote, since his business expansion was to be in continental Europe. Andorra was too inaccessible. Monte Carlo was a possibility. So also – excepting the fact of a 20 per cent income tax – was Jersey, in the Channel Islands. When one came to look at the problem more closely, it became apparent that he did not really need the facilities offered by these tax havens. What he really needed was a country which would welcome a new taxpayer, let him receive and pay tax on a reasonable salary, and not be concerned about some offshore structure, with which he and his family might be connected, and which could serve as the base for expanding his fortune.

Fiscal and other considerations produced a short list of three European countries – Austria, Belgium and Switzerland. The one which Mr X finally chose was Switzerland. His professional advisers here were able to discuss his position in advance with the tax authorities in the Cantons which they judged most likely to give a favourable ruling, and choose the one where the terms seemed most attractive.

Before his departure, Mr X obtained Treasury consent for the change of residence of his manufacturing company ('OldCo'), and rented an apartment in Switzerland. Upon his departure, he ceased immediately to be resident in the United Kingdom for income tax and, dependent upon his remaining non-resident for the full three years, ordinarily resident for capital gains tax. He would not be free of U.K. capital transfer tax for three years, but subject to that, he was at liberty to rearrange his affairs without any U.K. tax consequences. He would not become a Swiss resident until he had made his official application and the application had been granted. At this point, he dwelt in a kind of fiscal limbo, which had the merit at least that he was at liberty to re-arrange his affairs without any Swiss tax consequence.

Since Mr X was at any rate on his way to acquiring a non-U.K. domicil for capital transfer tax purposes, his assets ought not to be represented by shares in a company incorporated in England, but by shares in a company incorporated outside the United Kingdom, which, after the expiration of the three-year period, would rank as 'excluded property' for capital transfer tax. Accordingly, a company was incorporated in Jersey. This was to serve as a holding company ('HoldCo' in the diagram on p. 121) and a vehicle for the acquisition, in due course, of shares in other companies. It was a 'corporation tax' company in Jersey, and not liable to any tax there on its income.

As part of the reorganisation, HoldCo formed two companies, both Guernsey 'corporation tax' companies – 'PropCo' and 'NewCo'. The intended function of Newco was to take over the business of OldCo: it would be fully liable to U.K. corporation tax on its profits arising in the United Kingdom, but, not being resident there, would be at liberty to declare dividends without incurring any liability to advance corporation tax. NewCo had a very small share capital. It borrowed from a U.K. bank, and used the money to purchase the stock, work in progress and equipment of OldCo. OldCo (which would, in due course, be wound up) lent its money to HoldCo, which in turn made a 'back-to-back' deposit with the bank. NewCo would obtain tax relief for the interest it paid, while the corresponding interest would be paid to HoldCo free of U.K. tax. For this deduction to be of value to NewCo, it would have itself to make the profits of the business. NewCo therefore needed to acquire from OldCo the goodwill of its business.

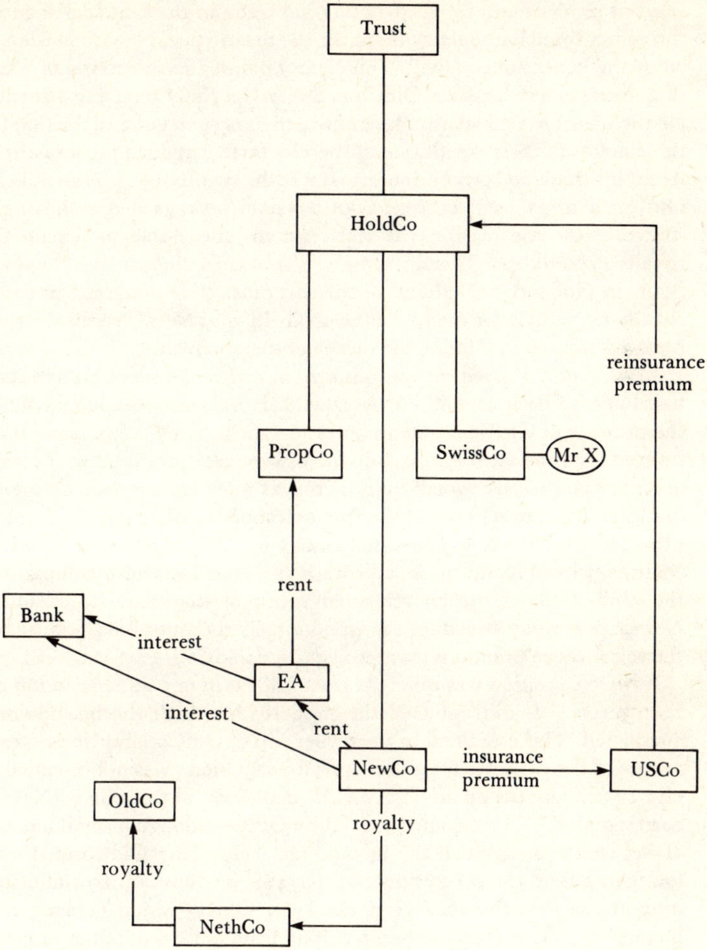

A U.K. *émigré*'s corporate structure

If OldCo had sold its goodwill immediately, it would have been liable to tax on its capital gain. That potential liability would cease only if OldCo could postpone its sale until a tax year in which (*a*) it was not resident and (*b*) it carried on no trade in the United Kingdom through a branch or agency there. In the meanwhile, NewCo needed to enjoy the benefit of goodwill. This clearly pointed to some kind of licensing arrangement between OldCo and NewCo, NewCo paying a royalty for the use of the goodwill. NewCo would expect to get a deduction for the amount of these royalties and thereby further reduce the amount of its profits liable to corporation tax. But if the royalty were receivable by OldCo, it might well be that OldCo would be regarded as having a source of income in the United Kingdom, and liable to tax on the royalty accordingly. This dilemma was solved by the use of a Stepping Stone in Holland – 'NethCo' in the diagram: NewCo agreed to pay a royalty to NethCo for the use of the goodwill, and NethCo paid a corresponding royalty to OldCo, the owner of the goodwill.

NewCo now carried on the business in much the same fashion as it had hitherto been carried on by OldCo. It did, however, depart from the practice of OldCo in one important respect. OldCo had never been insured for product liability. But there were real possibilities of claims arising from defective goods, and there was some logic in NewCo taking out insurance cover, since it was a much more thinly capitalised enterprise and to that extent less able to carry its own risks than OldCo had been. NewCo took out a policy with a specialist insurance company in the United States, which reinsured much of the risk with HoldCo; NewCo was able to deduct the premium in computing its profits, but the reinsurance premium was received by HoldCo free of tax.

NewCo's position was different from OldCo in one other, and important, respect. It did not own the property in which the business was conducted. This remained in the ownership of OldCo, and NewCo took a lease of the property from OldCo. This step alone was not intended to give rise to any tax advantage, for the deduction obtainable by NewCo corresponded to the income received by OldCo (though a small amount of tax would be saved if the income tax payable by OldCo were at a lower rate than the corporation tax payable by NewCo). By the beginning of the next financial year, however, OldCo would no longer be liable to tax on the capital gain resulting from a disposal of the property (since it would no longer carry on any trade in the United Kingdom) and PropCo might buy the property from OldCo at full market value, using for the purpose money borrowed from a U.K. bank. The diagram anticipates these events, and shows PropCo's estate agent ('EA') receiving rent from NewCo and paying interest to the bank on the money borrowed to pay the purchase price to OldCo. Once again, OldCo lent its money to HoldCo, which deposited it with the bank; the diagram shows a second amount of interest paid to HoldCo, being the interest on this amount. The net effect of this transaction was that NewCo was able to obtain a deduction in computing its U.K. profits, in respect of the rent paid for the property, while a substantial part of that amount indirectly accrued to HoldCo free of tax.

These were all the steps which Mr X needed to take in order to minimise the exposure of his new group of companies to United Kingdom taxes. But he contemplated one further step, which would not so much deal with the problem as take advantage of an opportunity. By going to Switzerland with the intention of making it his permanent home, he ceased to be domiciled in England, and after three years his change of domicil would become effective for U.K. capital transfer tax. But if he were to return to live in England, however late in life, his English domicil of origin would immediately revive, and any disposition of his HoldCo shares thereafter would attract capital transfer tax. However, if, after the expiry of the three years and before his return, he were to make a settlement of these shares, then these shares (and any other non-U.K. assets in the settlement) would retain their immunity from capital transfer tax, even though he might return to the United Kingdom, and even though the settlement were revocable or partly (or largely) for his own benefit during his lifetime. Mr X had no plans to return to the United Kingdom, but wanted to leave his options open, and conceived that such a settlement would be most desirable for this purpose.

From a Swiss point of view, such a settlement was also desirable. Once he became a resident there, he would become liable to an annual wealth tax, and this need not extend to assets which are not his, but held in a trust outside Switzerland. It was therefore desirable that such a settlement should come into existence before he became, in Swiss eyes, resident in Switzerland. And he ought not to make the settlement after he became a resident there, for another reason also: the Swiss have a gift tax of their own, and there would be little virtue in incurring an immediate and certain liability to Swiss gift tax, in order to avoid a future and uncertain liability to U.K. capital transfer tax.

The dilemma here seemed absolute: for Swiss purposes, the settlement had to be made straight away; for U.K. purposes, it must be postponed for three years. In the end, a solution was devised: Mr X was able to make an immediate settlement of which he was the tenant for life (so that no U.K. capital transfer tax liability arose), but crystallising the gift for Swiss purposes (at a time before he was resident there). After the expiry of the three-year period, this settlement would be revoked, and a fresh settlement made at a time when he would no longer be domiciled in the United Kingdom for capital transfer tax.

Mr X's activity in Switzerland was not a manufacturing activity, but a management one. He, together with a small staff, developed a facility to monitor the performance of the group's business in the United Kingdom, and to search for and make acquisition of new businesses. For this purpose, Mr X formed a Swiss company. For its services the Swiss company charged a fee to NewCo (and later to the companies subsequently acquired). These fees covered the office outgoings and provided the salary for Mr X – on which he paid Swiss tax.

It will be seen that there are three companies in the diagram which require to be resident outside the jurisdictions in which they are incorporated: HoldCo, PropCo and NewCo must each be managed and controlled outside the United Kingdom, and, if the proposed changes are made in the U.K. law, must have their place of effective management outside the United Kingdom: HoldCo must be managed and controlled outside Jersey, and PropCo and NewCo outside Guernsey. For this purpose, it is not necessary to make elaborate arrangements for board meetings to be held and minuted in places where, but for tax considerations, they would never have been held. Mr X was the true guiding spirit of all these companies, and his presence at, and contributions to, board meetings was real and vitally important, and it seemed quite unarguable that any of these companies should be regarded as resident in the United Kingdom or the Channel Islands.

Notes

1 Residence

1. Since the United States imposes tax on its citizens, wherever resident, anyone of substance contemplating becoming a U.S. citizen must consider very carefully the consequences of so doing.
2. It is advantageous for Dutch and Australian residents working abroad to suffer a low rate of income tax on their remuneration. They may consider employment by a Cyprus company, so that they suffer Cyprus tax at the maximum rate of 6 per cent. Such employment may also be advantageous for Austrian, Belgian, French, German and Swedish residents.
3. Consent may be required under Income and Corporation Taxes Act 1970, section 482. See p. 34 and Note 18 on p. 129. By contrast, a non-resident subsidiary of a U.K. company may do well to become resident in the United Kingdom before declaring dividends (see Income and Corporation Taxes Act 1970, section 256): legislation to counteract this manoeuvre has been promised but not yet introduced.
4. See p. 135, Note 1. Where a trading trust in the U.K. has a large profit in one or two years, one may consider the use of a commodity straddle in connection with a change of residence, the trustee taking the loss during the period of residence, but making the profit after the change of residence.
5. On leaving Canada there is a deemed realisation of all property which is not the listed shares of public companies. This produces a capital gains tax to the emigrant unless he is moving to a country with which Canada has a treaty that exempts capital gains. In that event he may elect to postpone the payments of the Canadian tax until the actual realisation of the assets which he can time to take place after he has moved to the jurisdiction which has a treaty with Canada that would exempt him from Canadian capital gains tax since he would be a resident of the other jurisdiction and not Canada. (Note that a waiting period may be required.)
6. An individual in these circumstances may contemplate a limited sojourn in the United States. He may during that time accumulate the income of his non-U.S. assets in an offshore trust.

7. Where the old jurisdiction is the United Kingdom, the result will be different – and generally less advantageous to the taxpayer – if he ceases to carry on the trade or profession or otherwise ceases to have the source of income: see Income and Corporation Taxes Act 1970, Part VI, Ch. II.
8. The tests of 'residence' for taxes on capital gains are not always the same as those affecting income tax. In the United Kingdom, exemption from capital gains tax is afforded to individuals only if they are not 'ordinarily resident' – which in practice requires a continuous period of three fiscal years of non-residence. Exception is made for those who work abroad full time for at least a whole tax year. One way of overcoming the three-year problem is to spend one tax year in a suitable country which has a tax treaty with the United Kingdom, under which residents of that country are exempt from U.K. capital gains tax. For this purpose it is not necessary for the individual to cease to be resident *in* the United Kingdom so long as he is a resident *of* the other country for treaty purposes. The choice of countries, however, is not wide. Not every treaty provides exemption from capital gains tax, and, naturally, the taxpayer does not want to become a resident of a country which would impose its own capital gains tax on his disposal. Three countries appear to satisfy both conditions; Sweden and Spain do not impose tax on all capital gains; in Canada a new resident has an uplifted base cost (so that the only gain liable to tax in Canada is that which reflects an increase in value since the date of his arrival).
9. In the United Kingdom, capital transfer tax is levied on those domiciled there, and a U.K.-domiciled individual requires three years of foreign domicil before his potential liability to the tax ceases (see Finance Act 1975, section 45). He may protect himself during the interim period by acquiring a domicil in France: see Articles 2 and 5 of the United Kingdom/France Estate Duty Treaty.

2 Source

1. See, in detail, Edo de Vries, *The Taxation of Non-residents* (London, 1983).
2. Switzerland, unexpectedly, is the most conspicuous exception to this generalisation, though bankers there have for many years utilised the 'fiduciary deposit' to overcome this competitive disadvantage.
3. Presently 52 per cent (on profits over £500,000 per annum) and 30 per cent respectively: Finance Act 1972, sections 93 and 95, as amended.
4. Bank of America publishes an excellent pamphlet on Captives, mostly from the pen of Sidney Pine, whose pioneering work in this field is well known.

5. The Taxes Management Act 1970, section 82 exonerates a U.K. agent from liability for the tax, but the principal remains liable.
6. That is, a company fully liable to tax in Luxembourg, not a Holding Company. See p. 72, and Note 14 on p. 137.

3 The United Kingdom

1. The United Kingdom taxes less heavily than many of the other twenty-three O.E.C.D. countries: in 1981 it came tenth on the list.
2. Except on business assets; see Capital Gains Tax Act 1979, section 12, and Income and Corporation Taxes Act 1970, section 246.
3. The question of control is one of fact: the fact that the executive officers reside outside the United Kingdom and that board meetings are held outside the United Kingdom does not exclude the possibility that such meetings merely rubber-stamp decisions taken elsewhere, for example by the board of the parent company meeting in London: see *Bullock* v. *Unit Construction Co.* (18 T.C. 712).
4. Territories which have historical ties with Britain generally have this feature in their tax law – see the list of territories under the heading 'Non-resident Companies' in Appendix 1 (paragraph 4). It is understood that Singapore no longer permits the incorporations of non-resident trading companies (the more adventurous may care to explore the possibilities of Botswana, Swaziland and Malaysia). It has been abolished elsewhere, for example, in Canada and in the Republic of Ireland.
5. See Note 2 above.
6. The writer knows of one United Kingdom treaty where no request for information has ever been made by either party! While this may be regarded as exceptional, the author has never personally come across a case in which any information relating to the ultimate ownership of a non-resident company has been divulged by the tax authorities in the United Kingdom to those of any other country. There seems to be a general feeling that the provisions for exchange of information are likely to be invoked more frequently in the future; but one has to bear in mind that the Revenue is empowered to require information only for the purpose of assessing liability to United Kingdom tax and does not have power to require information simply for the purpose of communicating it to other tax authorities in accordance with the terms of a tax treaty (cf. the position in the United States: *U.S.* v. *A. L. Burbank & Co. Ltd.* C.A. 25 25 F2d 9).
7. From the beginning of the Second World War until 1979, the United Kingdom had a system of exchange control restricting transfers of money and other assets outside what used to be called the 'Sterling Area' – properly, the Scheduled Territories. Exchange control has now been indefinitely suspended but there is from time to time talk of its return, and it may therefore be helpful to describe

how non-resident companies were affected by it – on the not unreasonable assumption that if these controls return, they will take a similar form.

A company was treated as non-resident for exchange control purposes if the beneficial ownership of the shares were vested in (or held on trust for) persons resident outside the Scheduled Territories, though the identity of those persons might be reserved to a telephone conversation – in which case they were not referred to by name in official correspondence. The permitted activities of the company could extend to most kinds of trading and investment, but the company was not allowed to carry on business as a trustee or as a life insurance company or otherwise be involved in investing or dealing with funds belonging to others, nor was approval given in advance for transactions in real estate or commodity futures in the Scheduled Territories. The shares in the company were required to be denominated in a currency other than sterling – and, for some inscrutable reason, other than Swiss francs.

8. The proposed new section read as follows:

1 (1) After the coming into force of this section, a company shall be regarded for the purposes of the Tax Acts as resident or not resident in the United Kingdom according as the place from which the management of the company's business as a whole is conducted is or is not in the United Kingdom; and, accordingly, if that place differs from the place where the central management and control of the company's business is exercised, the latter place shall no longer be taken into account for those purposes.

(2) In the case of a company where the functions of management are exercised in different places, the place which is relevant for the purposes of subsection (1) above is the place from which is conducted the immediate day to day management of the business as a whole (as distinct from any higher or supervisory level of management on the one hand and the management of part only of the company's business on the other).

(3) References in subsections (1) and (2) above to the company's business are references to those trading or other activities which principally constitute the company's business.

(4) For the purposes of the Tax Acts, a company which is being wound up or which is no longer carrying on any business shall be regarded as continuing to be resident in the United Kingdom if it was so resident for those purposes immediately before any of its activities came under the control of the liquidator or, as the case may be, before it ceased to carry on business.

9. Not Hong Kong or Singapore, which have estate duties of their own. Alternatively, the English company may issue share warrants to bearer and the holder keep his warrants outside the United Kingdom. Such shares and warrants have a foreign *situs*, and accordingly, in the hands of a non-domiciled individual, are

'excluded property' for U.K. capital transfer tax: Finance Act 1975, section 24.

10. The income is subject to income tax at the basic rate of 30 per cent plus 15 per cent surcharge (Finance Act 1973, section 16). Contrast the 'Interest in Possession' trust, discussed in the text.
11. Rather different considerations applied for exchange control. As mentioned earlier, the Bank of England used not in practice to designate a company non-resident if it was formed to carry on a trust business. But where a trust was created with non-sterling funds by a settlor residing outside the Sterling Area, the trust was treated as non-resident. As a practical matter, then, one achieved freedom from exchange control by having the trust company treated as resident in general terms, but as a non-resident in its capacity as trustee of that particular trust.
12. Income and Corporation Taxes Act 1970, section 238(2).
13. Income and Corporation Taxes Act 1970, section 122(2). The subsection refers to a person who satisfies the Revenue that *he* is non-domiciled. The statements in the text require 'he' to be read as 'it' when the *person* is a company.
14. United Kingdom/France Treaty, Article 12.
15. United Kingdom/Ireland Treaty, Article 13.
16. For example, under the Netherlands treaty, the effective mainstream corporation tax rate of a Dutch company's U.K. subsidiary may be as little as 43 per cent.
17. See Income and Corporation Taxes Act 1970, sections 115–118. The 'previous-year' basis gives rise to many anomalies. A U.K.-resident partner in a foreign partnership, for example, is taxable on the share to which he is entitled in a fiscal year of profits arising in the basis period ending in the previous fiscal year. Where in the meanwhile there has been a change in his partnership share, he may pay on less (or more) than what he has received.
18. Where:

    (*a*) the body corporate resident in the United Kingdom is incorporated after the passing of the Act for the purpose of carrying on a new trade or business not theretofore carried on by any person; and

    (*b*) more than fifty per cent of the issued share capital of that body corporate in existence at the time of the transactions in question, or, if there is then in existence issued share capital of the body corporate of more than one class, more than fifty per cent of the issued share capital thereof of each class is then, and was when it was issued, in the beneficial ownership of persons not ordinarily resident in the United Kingdom.

    But see the proposals for the repeal of section 482, Note 8 *supra*.
19. See *Williams* v. *Singer* (7 T.C. 419).
20. The United Kingdom is not on the list of countries to which payments by Australian residents require Reserve Bank approval.

21. Article 13.
22. But this does not affect his right to the 'remittance basis' for income tax and capital gains tax. It is important for a person intending to take advantage of this regime to maintain the 'outward and visible signs' of his foreign domicil – the grave space, the will, the associations and other links with the community in the country of his domicil, and the citizenship or other legal right to carry into effect his intention ultimately to return to that country. Much may turn also on the kind of statements he makes to the press, the Home Office, and – of course – the Revenue.

4 Low-tax Jurisdictions

1. The principal features of these jurisdictions were described in 1969 in the first edition of the writer's *Tax Havens* (now M. Grundy and J. Walters, *Grundy's Tax Havens*, 4th edition, London, 1983); now see also W. H. and D. B. Diamond, *Tax Havens of the World* (New York, 1976), M. Langer, *Practical International Tax Planning* (New York, 1979), and B. Spitz, *Tax Haven Encyclopaedia* (London, 1983). These jurisdictions are listed under 'Zero-Tax Jurisdictions' in Appendix 1.
2. Similar facilities are available in Freeport, Grand Bahama.
3. Foreign income of residents of Malaysia or Singapore is taxable only if remitted there (though the Singapore tax authorities claim – with what jurisdiction it is hard to see – to be entitled to tax foreign income of non-residents if the income is remitted there). A similar rule applies to individuals and companies resident in the British Virgin Islands but not domiciled (in the case of companies, not incorporated) there (see p. 46). This 'remittance basis' has, of course, its origin in the U.K. system – see p. 30. Whereas the British Virgin Islands imposes no tax on outgoing dividends, both Malaysia and Singapore have a system of charging tax on dividends similar to that in force in the United Kingdom before 1965: the dividend tax is satisfied by the income tax on the company's profit, but only up to the amount of the income tax actually charged down to the date of the dividend. The result is that a tax charge arises where a company declares dividends out of unremitted foreign income, and a similar charge would arise if the foreign income were treated as distributed.

   Malaysia and Singapore are parties to a number of treaties, and companies resident there may obtain the benefit of reduced taxes under some (but not all) treaties while paying no local tax because the income is not remitted. Contrast the position in Brunei, where the provisions of the Income Tax Enactment (of 1949) imposing a similar charge on distributions have never been brought into effect (paragraph (*b*) of the First Schedule).
4. The Principality is well known to be a tax haven, and that perhaps

is its main disadvantage. Otherwise it satisfies all the criteria of an excellent tax haven: it is stable and efficient; it has its own company and trust law; its currency is the Swiss franc. It boasts a unique institution – the Establishment, generally known by its German name, the *Anstalt*. An *Anstalt* may be more like a company or more like a trust or something in between, depending on how its constitution is framed: an *Anstalt* may be formed like a company, the founder retaining all the rights which in a company would be vested in shareholders, and able to assign these rights if he wishes; or it may be formed like a trust with no founder's rights, and in that case the *Anstalt* is controlled by a board, and administered for the benefit of its beneficiaries, in accordance with the terms of its articles or by-laws.

5. See Appendix 2.
6. Of up to 17 per cent and 15 per cent respectively.
7. The Act incorporates many of the recommendations of Dickerson in his *Proposals for a New Business Corporations Law for Canada*, 1971.
8. Cyprus does not tax profits of ships registered under the Cyprus flag, of offshore partnerships composed of aliens, of branches of foreign and foreign-owned companies engaged in activities outside Cyprus, of offshore banking units, or of trusts with foreign settlors, beneficiaries and trust property. It imposes tax at the rate of 4.25 per cent on the 'Offshore' Company (that is, one doing business outside Cyprus and owned by aliens, even though incorporated and managed and controlled in Cyprus), with no withholding tax on dividends, but no credit for foreign tax. Cyprus does not impose estate duty on shares owned by aliens in Cyprus shipping or Offshore Companies: see generally, C. Demetriades, *Cyprus in International Tax Planning* (London, 1980).
9. Exempted Companies in Cayman and in Turks and Caicos enjoy exemptions from future tax (see pp. 64 and 66 respectively). But what an Exempt Company in Gibraltar enjoys is an exemption, both as regards profits and as regards distributions, from tax presently imposed. In addition, shares in and debts of Exempt Companies are exempt from estate duty in Gibraltar.

   To form an Exempt Company, it is necessary to make application to the Financial Secretary and give him certain information – information which he is bound to treat as confidential. He has power to refuse exemption, but in practice exemption will be granted where the proposed transactions involve nothing unlawful or improper. A certificate of exemption is valid for twenty-five years, subject to payment of the annual fee of £225. Changes of beneficial ownership of the shares have to be approved by Government; but this requirement does not apply to the acquisition by transfer or sale or by any other means of an interest by a new or substituted beneficiary under a trust. Bearer Shares and coupons may be issued, but the certificates must be deposited with a bank.

In practice the Gibraltar exempt company has been used for many years for very much the same kind of transactions as are conducted by non-resident companies in the Channel Islands, the Isle of Man or the United Kingdom. In those territories, exemption from tax is dependent upon the company not being managed and controlled there, and not carrying on its trade there. Non-resident companies may also be formed in Gibraltar (for which the annual fee is £200), and must satisfy the same criteria to be exempt from local tax. But the freedom from tax enjoyed by an Exempt Company depends neither on its place of management nor on the place at which its trade is carried on, and accordingly Gibraltar has the advantage that directors' meetings may be held there, and trade carried on there – in the fullest sense, including the establishment of an office or other visible place of business.

Gibraltar has now extended its Exempt Company status to companies incorporated outside Gibraltar (for which the annual fee is £500). For such companies it has the advantage over Monaco that the establishment of an office and the conduct of normal business activity does not result in any exposure to tax there (cf. the position in Monaco, discussed in Note 16 below).

More recently, Gibraltar has introduced a catagory of 'Qualifying Companies'. The Income Tax (Amendment) Ordinance 1983, effective from 1 July 1983, permits companies which would qualify for exempt status to opt, as an alternative to payment of the fixed annual tax, for payment of a reduced form of income tax at the rate of 2 per cent or 27 per cent (depending on whether or not profits are remitted to Gibraltar).

The text of the Exempt Company legislation is reproduced in Appendix 5.

10. Companies cannot generally change their domicil, that is, their place of incorporation. However, provision for such change is made in the laws of some other jurisdictions – in Bermuda, Canada (provinces of Ontario and New Brunswick), Cook Islands, Liechtenstein (with Government approval), Nauru, Netherlands Antilles, Netherlands (to and from the Antilles), Panama, Seychelles, Switzerland, Turks and Caicos and Vanuatu.
11. See Note 8 *supra*.
12. See p. 64 and p. 66.
13. For Captive Insurance Companies, see p. 58.
14. For the relevance of foreign partnerships to persons resident but not domiciled in the United Kingdom, see p. 32. For the merits of Swiss and U.S. partnerships see pp. 69–70.
15. See p. 24.
16. It is necessary to distinguish between three kinds of office which a foreign company may have in Monaco. The first kind is the ordinary branch office which carries on a normal business activity and which is taxed at the rate of 35 per cent of the profits derived from its

local activity. The second is the administrative office, which does not open its door to the public but performs administrative or other services in furtherance of a business activity which takes place abroad. In such a case, the profits of the business activity are not taxable in Monaco, but a notional profit is attributable to the local office and taxed at the rate of 35 per cent. The tax authorities have for many years adopted the rule of thumb that 8 per cent of the local expenses of the Monaco office be treated as the local profit.

Either of these two kinds of office require Government permission. It seems that a number of offices which were authorised purely as administrative offices have been found in fact to be engaged in business operations, which properly puts them into the higher tax bracket, and it has therefore now become the practice of the tax authorities in Monaco to enquire more closely into the location of the business activities.

The third type of office, which is perhaps not truly an 'office' at all, is the office maintained for a quite different purpose, that is, for the purpose of establishing 'management and control' of for example a Guernsey company or an English company. Management services are provided by Monegasque companies for a fee. The taxation consequence of this arrangement is that the Monegasque management company is taxed at 35 per cent on the profits resulting from the fee it charges, but the foreign company will not itself be liable to any Monegasque tax, nor will it be brought in to the French exchange control net, provided its business activity takes place outside Monaco and also outside France.

Those of the staff who reside in the Principality will enjoy the freedom from personal income tax which is a signal feature of Monaco – though social security contributions are significant, property is expensive and the cost of living is high (value added tax being payable as in France). French citizens remain liable to tax in their own country.

17. The first move to encourage foreign companies to set up office in Greece came in 1961. These provisions, substantially amended in 1982, are still in force, and they exempt 'technical companies' from Greek tax, so long as they are engaged exclusively in activities whose objects lie outside Greece. Typically, a company engaged in construction work in the Middle East may have an office in Athens to manage these operations. If a company is to take advantage of this exemption, at least 80 per cent of its personnel must be Greek, it must lodge a bank guarantee of U.S. $50,000, and it must import a minimum amount of foreign currency to cover its operating expenses, the minimum being U.S. $12,000 for each foreign employee.

In 1967 the military regime provided for this exemption to be extended to a commercial or industrial company on condition that it imports a minimum amount of foreign exchange each year. Like the technical companies which benefit from the 1961 law, the objects of such a company must lie outside Greece. Typically a company with factories in Africa and the Middle East will base skilled personnel in Athens or Piraeus, from which they can conveniently fly to Cairo, Beirut or Teheran. The company is exempt from all tax on its income and profits and may import equipment for the office and for the homes of foreign personnel (including one car per family) without customs duty.

5 Zero-Tax Jurisdictions

1. See J. Walters (ed.), *Grundy's Tax Havens* (4th edition, London 1983).
2. For onshore companies, it has always (except in exceptional circumstances) been necessary to have 51 per cent local equity. Partnerships must be 100 per cent local (a partnership has corporate personality on the French model). Exempt companies, on the other hand, may be formed without any Bahraini capital at all, and these are the companies which one would normally envisage as 'tax-haven' companies. They are not allowed to carry on business in Bahrain.
3. That is, in what is essentially an English form. The company's powers are limited by the objects set out in its memorandum of association. The duration of the company is indefinite.
4. All these territories were formerly part of the Sterling Area (later, the 'Scheduled Territories') but exchange control remains only in Bermuda and the Bahamas. It is broadly on the lines of that in force in the United Kingdom before October 1979. 'Non-resident' status is accorded to companies belonging to and trusts established by persons resident outside the territory, provided they in effect do no local business. Such companies and trusts are in effect outside the local exchange control, and will not be concerned with it unless they wish to do business with local residents, or to acquire local property or local currency.
5. See p. 17.
6. Listed in Appendix 1.
7. In Gibraltar and Seychelles the exemption is primarily an exemption from tax. In Cayman and in Turks and Caicos it is an exemption from certain requirements of the Companies Law.
8. By contrast, A. Vernay, in *Les Paradis Fiscaux* (Paris, 1968) advances the view that tax havens – most of which are members of the British Commonwealth or under powerful United States influence – are part of the mechanism whereby *la Wall Street* and *la City* impose upon the world '*La hégémonie anglo-saxonne*'.
9. See p. 131–2, Note 9.
10. A circumstance which may help a U.K.-resident individual to pray in aid the provisions of subsection (3) of Income and Corporation Taxes Act 1970, section 478.

11. Income Tax (Suspension) Ordinance 1977. Death Duties, by contrast, were abolished (Death Duties (Abolition) Ordinance 1977) though exchange control has been effectively suspended rather than abolished (Exchange Control (Scheduled Territories and General Exemption) Order 1976).
12. See p. 138, Note 1.

6 Tax Treaties

1. *Lord Strathalmond* v. *I.R.C.* (48 T.C. 537), approved in *I.R.C.* v. *Exxon* [1982] S.T.C. 356. An individual not abroad long enough to be not ordinarily resident in the United Kingdom may nevertheless be exempt from capital gains tax as a resident of a treaty country, and similar principles may apply to domicil and capital transfer tax. (See p. 126, Note 8.) Trustees resident in a treaty country but administering a trust wholly or partly in the United Kingdom may be exempt from capital gains tax without 'infecting' their beneficiaries (Finance Act 1981, section 80).
2. Treasury regulation 509122 purports to deny the benefit of the U.S. treaty to partnerships whose partners are not themselves entitled to treaty benefit.
3. See p. 35.
4. That is, which is entitled to the 'participation privilege' – see p. 50.
5. Article 10(3) of the Netherlands/U.K. Treaty. It is submitted that the use of a trust might provide the kind of 'control' permitted by paragraph (*d*).

   An alternative structure for avoiding ACT may be to have the profit-making activity carried on, not by a U.K.-resident company, but by a U.K. branch of a non-resident company; and this may be particularly advantageous where (because, for example, of capital allowances or carry-forward of losses) a U.K. company would not pay enough mainstream corporation tax to frank the advance corporation tax on intended dividends.
6. See p. 51.
7. The treaty permits the Antilles company to discontinue the net-basis election in the year of sale. There used to be other ways for non-resident aliens to avoid the U.S. tax consequences of disposing of their real estate investments in the United States – the instalment sale, the like kind exchange, the sale coupled with liquidation, or the sale of shares. The benefit of all these devices – including that of the treaty – has been ended by the Foreign Investment in Real Property Taxes Act ('FIRPTA'). It is still important for the non-resident alien investor to utilise a foreign company, so as to eliminate his potential exposure to U.S. gift and estate taxes. He will now think in terms of building up interest charges and other deductions to produce net operating losses in his company; if his company is established in a country which has made with the United States a

treaty of friendship, commerce and navigation containing an applicable non-discrimination provision, the company may elect, within ninety days after the purchase of the property, to be treated in the same way as a domestic corporation, so that on liquidation the tax rate is reduced to 20 per cent. It may still be possible for the investor to take his profit by way of a sale of shares – though the profit will now be smaller, because the purchaser will require a discount, reflecting the company's ultimate liability to FIRPTA. In some cases, the investor may adopt the 'Zimbabwe Solution': if he has real estate in some other country, with a base cost significantly higher than its present market value, he may acquire his U.S. investment by way of a 'like kind exchange', with the consequence that his high base cost is transferred to his U.S. property.

8. See p. 49.
9. See p. 131, Note 8.
10. See p. 47.
11. Barbados is one of the countries listed in the Canadian Income Tax Regulations, section 5907(11).
12. Article 55(1) of the Federal Direct Income Tax law exempts from Federal tax the profits of a foreign branch of a Swiss company and a similar exemption is granted by the equivalent Cantonal statutes. However, the profits of the branch are brought into computation for the purpose of calculating the rate of Swiss tax applicable on other (taxable) profits, if any.

    The U.S.–Swiss treaty allows the U.S. to tax profits of the branch of a Swiss company only to the extent that those profits are derived from a U.S. source. The treaty is currently being renegotiated and the U.S. is hoping to eliminate this particular anomaly.
13. Holland functions as an excellent Stepping Stone for interest and royalties, these items being received free of withholding taxes under the protection of various treaties and paid out free of withholding taxes. The tax administration normally requires that the Dutch Stepping Stone be left with a spread or turn of not less than ¼ per cent to ⅛ per cent of the loan or 2 per cent to 10 per cent of the royalties received; on this Dutch tax will be payable. It is always advisable to obtain a ruling, though the Dutch tax authorities may impose other conditions as a term of giving a ruling. Perhaps the main disadvantage of the Netherlands is that this function has by now become rather too well known, but tax administrations in other countries appear to tolerate it so long as the Stepping Stone company is independent of and acts at arm's length with its licensor and licensee or lender and borrower, and indeed in such circumstances the Dutch authorities themselves appear to be content with a turn smaller than that which they would require of an in-house Stepping Stone.

    In the Netherlands/United Kingdom treaty, Article 11(6) reads:

> The provisions of this Article shall not apply if the debt-claim in respect of which the interest is paid was created or assigned mainly for the purpose of taking advantage of this Article and not for bona fide commercial reasons.

and Article 12(5):

> The provisions of this Article shall not apply if the right or property giving rise to royalties created or assigned mainly for the purpose of taking advantage of the Article are not bona fide commercial reasons.

It is submitted that the 'purposes' with which these paragraphs are concerned are those only of the parties to the loan or licence, those of any ultimate lender or head-licensor being immaterial. A U.K. company cannot, as can its U.S. counterpart, raise a Eurobond loan by incorporating a finance subsidiary in the Netherlands or in the Netherlands Antilles (whose U.K. treaty contains similar provisions).

14. Luxembourg Holding Companies do not benefit from the tax treaties to which Luxembourg is a party (see p. 52). A Stepping Stone in Luxembourg is an ordinary, taxpaying company: it can receive interest free of tax from Belgium, Ireland, the United Kingdom and the United States, and can pay interest gross to a tax-free vehicle. The practice is to leave a normal commercial profit, which, as a guide (and depending on the amounts involved), might be between $\frac{1}{16}$ and $\frac{1}{8}$ per cent, in the tax-paying company. A Luxembourg Holding Company may be used as the tax-free vehicle: in such a structure one has two Luxembourg companies – one paying tax on the $\frac{1}{16}$ to $\frac{1}{8}$ per cent and the other a Holding Company, receiving (and, if required, accumulating) interest free of tax.

15. In the United Kingdom, the freedom from withholding tax on the outgoing payment is dependent upon the use of a document under seal, on the basis that the outgoing payment does not have a U.K. source if the document is kept outside the United Kingdom, but it is understood that the Inland Revenue in the United Kingdom has recently thought fit to challenge the validity of this thesis, so that – for the present at any rate – the United Kingdom does not merit a high place in the list of jurisdictions available for Stepping Stones.

16. Royalties may be paid to Denmark free of withholding tax from Antigua, Austria, Barbados, Belgium, Belize, British Virgin Islands, Cyprus, Dominica, Falkland Islands, Faroe Islands, Finland, France, Gambia, Germany, Ghana, Hungary, Iceland, Irish Republic, Italy, Jamaica, Kiribati, Luxembourg, Malawi, Malta, Mauritius, Montserrat, Netherlands, Netherlands Antilles, Nigeria, Norway, Pakistan, Solomon Islands, Sierra Leone, Singapore, Seychelles, Sri Lanka, St Kitts, St Lucia, St Vincent, Sweden, Switzerland, Tuvalu,

Uganda, United Kingdom, United States, Zimbabwe and Yemen; 6 per cent withholding tax is suffered on royalties emanating from Spain; 10 per cent from Australia, Japan, New Zealand, Philippines, Poland, Portugal and Romania; 15 per cent from Canada, Israel, Korea, Thailand, Trinidad, Tunisia and Zambia; 20 per cent from Kenya and Tanzania; and 26 per cent from Brazil.

Negotiations for new treaties are in progress with Argentina, Bulgaria, Greece, Morocco and the USSR. Negotiations for the revision of existing treaties are in progress with Canada, Finland, France, Netherlands, Iceland, Italy, India, Nigeria, Norway, Pakistan, Singapore, Sweden, Sri Lanka, United Kingdom and United States.

Other jurisdictions may also be useful – e.g. Germany for interest, Canada for copyright royalties or for foreign currency interest (especially if originating in the United States). The U.S. 80/20 company is interesting in this connection. If more than 80 per cent of a U.S. corporation's income comes from non-U.S. source, then dividends and interest paid by that company will not be subject to U.S. withholding tax. Some international bond offerings by non-U.S. corporations have been made through a finance subsidiary organised in the United States – a form of interest 'Stepping Stone'.

17. A simple form of anti-treaty-shopping provision which is a feature of the present U.S./Netherlands Antilles treaty has been circumvented by the 'Dutch Sandwich' – the Antilles company owned by a Netherlands company in turn owned by an Antilles company.

7 Offshore Trusts

1. That is, the maximum permitted duration of the trust. Statutes in some jurisdictions (for example, the United Kingdom and the Cayman Islands) provide for the duration of a trust simply as a number of years. In the absence of such statutory provision, the perpetuity period is the duration of lives in being plus twenty-one years. The 'lives' need not be those of beneficiaries or anyone connected with the trust: in the British Commonwealth, the usual practice is to define the perpetuity period by reference to the lives of the descendants of a recently deceased monarch.
2. It is common to provide in a trust instrument that where all or any part of the capital of a corporation is included in the trust fund, the trustees shall not be bound to interfere in the management or conduct of the business of the corporation but shall be at liberty to leave the conduct of its business wholly to its directors or other officers. And it is commonly further provided that the trustees shall not be liable for any loss to the trust fund caused by any act or omission of the corporation or of any of its officers. It is doubtful to what extent, if any, such a provision is capable of

exonerating the trustees from their normal duty in relation to an investment of this kind – in particular their duty to receive an adequate flow of information concerning the intentions and activities of the board of the company, and to step in and stop the board from entering upon any unsuitable, hazardous or imprudent project. See the English decision of *Bartlett* v. *Barclays Bank Trust Co. Ltd.* [1980] 1 Ch. 515.

3. A good deal of drafting ingenuity has been devoted to perfecting a form of 'triggering clause', so that the place of administration, or the law of a trust, is changed upon the happening of certain events. The author has never seen a draft which he regards as wholly satisfactory; whether the emergency is of such a nature as to require the removal of trusts from a territory may be a matter for nice judgment in a particular case, and it seems a better practice to appoint an individual or a committee to make this judgment, rather than to attempt an impersonal mechanism to effect the change.
4. Would a purported change of law, from one which recognises trusts to one which does not, create a resulting trust in favour of the settlor? It is perhaps preferable to restrict the powers so that the settlement can be made subject to a new law only if the new law gives effect to trusts in the same manner as did the original law governing the settlement at the time when the settlement was made.
5. Some practitioners favour the creation of so-called 'vacuum trusts' – where the only beneficiaries named are charities, but the trustees are given power to add as beneficiaries any one or more persons of their choice. This is generally accompanied by undertakings by the trustees to add beneficiaries nominated by a particular individual. This may give rise to the dilemma that if such an undertaking is not part of the trust, the power itself may be void (see the English decision of *Blausten* v. *I.R.C.* [1972] Ch. 256), but if it is a term of the trust, the fiscal or other purpose of this manoeuvre will only be attained by concealing the fact.
6. To what extent should trustees in another jurisdiction enquire into the effect, under the personal law of the settlor, of the making of a settlement governed by the law of that other jurisdiction? It is submitted that where the effect of the settlor's personal law is that he lacks the capacity to make a settlement, the trustees will hold the trust fund of any purported settlement on a resulting trust for the settlor; however, where the settlor under his personal law has the capacity to make a settlement, but the effect of his so doing is to confer upon a wife or other dependants rights not conferred by the settlement, the Court would not enforce those rights against the trustee. Could an aggrieved wife or dependant obtain judgment against the trustee in the jurisdiction of the settlor's personal law, and then enforce that judgment in the trustees' jurisdiction?

7. Non-resident aliens wishing to benefit U.S. citizens or residents may do well to utilise a 'grantor trust'. The income of a 'grantor trust' is taxable on the grantor, not on the beneficiaries. This works to the advantage of the parties where the grantor is a non-resident alien, and the income has a non-U.S. source, but the beneficiaries are U.S. taxpayers. In these circumstances the beneficiaries receive non-taxable gifts. It may be desirable to use a trust with more than one individual grantor, or with a corporate grantor – so that the death of one individual does not cause the trust to cease to be a grantor trust.
8. See p. 71.
9. See pp. 69–71.
10. For example, a longer period of accumulation may be allowed in the Cayman Islands (see p. 67 and Appendix 3).
11. In Gibralter, this practice now has statutory force: Income Tax (Amendment) Ordinance 1983.

    The United States and its dependencies provide a similar freedom from tax on foreign-source income distributable to non-resident alien beneficiaries, but by a different route: distributable income may be deducted in computing the taxable income of the trust, but nevertheless retains in the hands of the beneficiary the character it had in the hands of the trustee. A similar benefit is again to be found in jurisdictions with a territorial basis of tax. It is no doubt for this reason that the practice referred to in the text is not required in Hong Kong (p. 42). A Panamanian trust is similarly free of tax on its foreign income. Panama has a trust law, which is presently in course of revision. New companies are incorporated in Panama at the astonishing rate of 120 a day. Whether their new trust law is destined for a comparable success seems doubtful: a practitioner asked to advise on a problem or dispute concerning an 'Anglo-Saxon' trust may turn to a variety of learned works and many years of precedents; no such assistance is available to his colleague in a civil law country.
12. See p. 32.
13. See p. 132, Note 10.
14. See pp. 5–13.

Index